Sebastian Weber

Structure and Dynamics of Networks

Sebastian Weber

Structure and Dynamics of Networks

Sheding light on the interplay of network topology and dynamics

Südwestdeutscher Verlag für Hochschulschriften

Impressum/Imprint (nur für Deutschland/ only for Germany)
Bibliografische Information der Deutschen Nationalbibliothek: Die Deutsche Nationalbibliothek verzeichnet diese Publikation in der Deutschen Nationalbibliografie; detaillierte bibliografische Daten sind im Internet über http://dnb.d-nb.de abrufbar.
Alle in diesem Buch genannten Marken und Produktnamen unterliegen warenzeichen-, marken- oder patentrechtlichem Schutz bzw. sind Warenzeichen oder eingetragene Warenzeichen der jeweiligen Inhaber. Die Wiedergabe von Marken, Produktnamen, Gebrauchsnamen, Handelsnamen, Warenbezeichnungen u.s.w. in diesem Werk berechtigt auch ohne besondere Kennzeichnung nicht zu der Annahme, dass solche Namen im Sinne der Warenzeichen- und Markenschutzgesetzgebung als frei zu betrachten wären und daher von jedermann benutzt werden dürften.

Verlag: Südwestdeutscher Verlag für Hochschulschriften Aktiengesellschaft & Co. KG
Dudweiler Landstr. 99, 66123 Saarbrücken, Deutschland
Telefon +49 681 37 20 271-1, Telefax +49 681 37 20 271-0, Email: info@svh-verlag.de
Zugl.: Darmstadt, Technische Universität, Dissertation, 2008

Herstellung in Deutschland:
Schaltungsdienst Lange o.H.G., Berlin
Books on Demand GmbH, Norderstedt
Reha GmbH, Saarbrücken
Amazon Distribution GmbH, Leipzig
ISBN: 978-3-8381-0719-6

Imprint (only for USA, GB)
Bibliographic information published by the Deutsche Nationalbibliothek: The Deutsche Nationalbibliothek lists this publication in the Deutsche Nationalbibliografie; detailed bibliographic data are available in the Internet at http://dnb.d-nb.de.
Any brand names and product names mentioned in this book are subject to trademark, brand or patent protection and are trademarks or registered trademarks of their respective holders. The use of brand names, product names, common names, trade names, product descriptions etc. even without a particular marking in this works is in no way to be construed to mean that such names may be regarded as unrestricted in respect of trademark and brand protection legislation and could thus be used by anyone.

Publisher:
Südwestdeutscher Verlag für Hochschulschriften Aktiengesellschaft & Co. KG
Dudweiler Landstr. 99, 66123 Saarbrücken, Germany
Phone +49 681 37 20 271-1, Fax +49 681 37 20 271-0, Email: info@svh-verlag.de

Copyright © 2009 by the author and Südwestdeutscher Verlag für Hochschulschriften Aktiengesellschaft & Co. KG and licensors
All rights reserved. Saarbrücken 2009

Printed in the U.S.A.
Printed in the U.K. by (see last page)
ISBN: 978-3-8381-0719-6

Abstract

Networks have become a general concept to model the structure of arbitrary relationships among entities. The framework of a network introduces a fundamentally new approach apart from 'classical' structures found in physics to model the topology of a system. In the context of networks fundamentally new topological effects can emerge and lead to a class of topologies which are termed 'complex networks'. The concept of a network successfully models the static topology of an empirical system, an arbitrary model, and a physical system. Generally networks serve as a host for some dynamics running on it in order to fulfill a function. The question of the reciprocal relationship among a dynamical process on a network and its topology is the context of this Thesis.

This context is studied in both directions. The network topology constrains or enhances the dynamics running on it, while the reciprocal interaction is of the same importance. Networks are commonly the result of an evolutionary process, e.g. protein interaction networks from biology. Within such an evolution the dynamics shapes the underlying network topology with respect to an optimal achievement of the function to perform. Answering the question what the influence on a dynamics of a particular topological property has requires the accurate control over the topological properties in question. In this Thesis the degree distribution, two-point correlations, and clustering are the studied topological properties. These are motivated by the ubiquitous presence and importance within almost all empirical networks. An analytical framework to measure and to control such quantities of networks along with numerical algorithms to generate them is developed in a first step. Networks with the examined topological properties are then used to reveal their impact on two rather general dynamics on networks. Finally, an evolution of networks is studied to shed light on the influence the dynamics has on the network topology.

Zusammenfassung

Netzwerke stellen einen allgemeinen Ansatz dar, die Struktur von beliebig miteinander verknüpften Einheiten zu modellieren. Das Konzept eines Netzwerkes ermöglicht die Abbildung von Strukturen, die sich grundlegend von ‚klassischen' Strukturen aus der Physik unterscheiden. So können durch Netzwerke neue topologische Effekte entstehen, welche eine besondere Klasse von Netzwerken darstellen und auch ‚komplexe Netzwerke' genannt werden. Im Allgemeinen modelliert ein Netzwerk die statische Topologie eines empirischen Systems, eines beliebigen Modells und eines physikalischen Systems. Im Gegensatz dazu ist eine auf dem Netzwerk ablaufende Dynamik verantwortlich für die Verrichtung einer Funktion des Netzwerkes. Der Zusammenhang von Topologie und Dynamik eines Netzwerkes ist Thema dieser Arbeit.

Die Topologie eines Netzwerkes bedingt die Eigenschaften einer darauf ablaufen Dynamik. Gleichzeitig aber beeinflusst die Dynamik die zugrunde liegende Topologie, da Netzwerke wie z.B. biologische Protein-Interaktionsnetzwerke das Resultat eines evolutionären Prozesses darstellen. Eine solche Netzwerkevolution wirkt auf die Topologie des Netzwerkes durch Selektion auf Basis der Dynamik. Die aufgeworfene Fragestellung bedingt folglich auch eine reziproke Untersuchung. Voraussetzung für eine Analyse des Einflusses von topologischen Eigenschaften auf einen dynamischen Prozess ist die präzise Kontrolle über die untersuchten Eigenschaft der Netzwerktopologie. In dieser Arbeit wird der Einfluss der Gradverteilung, Zweipunktkorrelationen und Clustering studiert. Diese Netzwerkeigenschaften sind durch die Präsenz in praktisch allen empirischen Netzwerken motiviert. Zunächst wird eine analytische Beschreibung dieser topologischen Eigenschaften eingeführt, sowie numerische Verfahren zur Erzeugung solcher Netzwerke vorgestellt. Daraufhin werden Netzwerke mit den fraglichen Eigenschaften genutzt, um ihre Wirkung auf zwei generische Dynamiken zu verstehen. Zur Analyse der Einflußnahme der Dynamik auf die Topologie eines Netzwerkes, wird eine durch die Dynamik getriebene Netzwerkevolution untersucht.

Contents

1	**Introduction**	**1**
2	**Structure of Complex Networks**	**7**
2.1	Network Description	7
2.2	Randomized Networks	10
	2.2.1 Uncorrelated Networks	11
	2.2.2 Two-Point Correlated Networks	11
	2.2.3 Two-Point Correlated Networks with Clustering	14
2.3	Finite Scale-Free Networks	15
2.4	Conclusion	20
3	**Dynamics on Complex Networks**	**21**
3.1	Reaction-Diffusion Process	22
	3.1.1 Analytical Results	23
	3.1.2 Comparing Network Topologies	26
	3.1.3 Two-Point Correlations	28
3.2	Prisoner's Dilemma	32
	3.2.1 Two-Point Correlations	41
	3.2.2 Clustering	44
3.3	Conclusion	44
4	**Evolution of Networks**	**47**
4.1	Network Mutation	47
	4.1.1 Configuration Model Scheme	49
	4.1.2 Copying Scheme	52
4.2	Network Selection by Dynamics	55
	4.2.1 Reaction-Diffusion Process	58
	4.2.2 Prisoner's Dilemma	63
4.3	Conclusion	67
5	**Conclusion and Discussion**	**71**
A	**Appendix**	**75**

	A.1	Analytical Treatment of the Annihilation-Diffusion Process	75
		A.1.1 Particle pair-correlations	76
		A.1.2 Density decay	77
		A.1.3 Validation of the approximations	79
	A.2	Numerical Methods	81
		A.2.1 Generation of Two-Point Correlated Networks	81
		A.2.2 Generation of Two-Point Correlated Networks with Clustering	84
		A.2.3 Annihilation-Diffusion Dynamics	85
		A.2.4 Prisoner's Dilemma Dynamics	86

Bibliography   **89**

List of Publications   **95**

Acknowledgements   **97**

List of Figures

2.1 Frequency distribution of a scale-free distribution, $\gamma = 2.5$ 16
2.2 $P(j \geq k)$ of scale-free distribution without and with $k_{\max} = 10^2$ . . . 16
2.3 $k_{\mathrm{nn}}(k)/\langle k \rangle$ of uncorrelated scale-free network with different $k_{\max}$ . . . 18

3.1 ρ^{-1} of $A + B \to \emptyset$ reaction on scale-free networks with varying γ . . . 26
3.2 ρ^{-1} of $A + B \to \emptyset$ reaction on scale-free networks with varying N . . 27
3.3 Pattern measures vs. ρ^{-1} of $A + B \to \emptyset$ reaction 29
3.4 Impact of two-point correlation on $A + B \to \emptyset$ reaction 31
3.5 Cooperator density for effective payoff Prisoner's Dilemma, $\gamma = 3$ . . 38
3.6 Average cooperator degree for effective payoff Prisoner's Dilemma . . 39
3.7 Cooperator density for effective payoff Prisoner's Dilemma, $\gamma = 2.5$. 41
3.8 Effective payoff Prisoner's Dilemma with two-point correlations . . . 42
3.9 Cumulative Prisoner's Dilemma with two-point correlations 42
3.10 Cumulative Prisoner's Dilemma with clustering, ρ 45
3.11 Cumulative Prisoner's Dilemma with clustering, C_c 45

4.1 Configuration model mutation scheme evaluation, $P(k)$ 50
4.2 Configuration model mutation scheme evaluation, r 51
4.3 Copy mutation scheme evaluation, $P(k)$ 53
4.4 Copy mutation scheme evaluation, r 54
4.5 Evaluation of combined fitness measure of $A + B \to \emptyset$ reaction 60
4.6 Evolution by $A + B \to \emptyset$ reaction, $P(k)$ and $P(j \geq k)$ 61
4.7 Evolution by $A + B \to \emptyset$ reaction, fitness measure and $\sigma_k/\overline{k}$ 62
4.8 Evolution by cumulative Prisoner's Dilemma, ρ and $\sigma_k/\overline{k}$ 64
4.9 Evolution by cumulative Prisoner's Dilemma, β^{-1} and $\overline{k}$ 65
4.10 Evolution by cumulative Prisoner's Dilemma, $P(k)$ and $P(j \geq k)$ . . 66

A.1 Characteristic degrees of $A + B \to \emptyset$ reaction 80
A.2 Evaluation of jamming term of $A + B \to \emptyset$ reaction for different γ . . 81
A.3 Evaluation of quasi-static approximation of $A + B \to \emptyset$ reaction . . . 82

List of Tables

4.1 Combined fitness for $A + B \to \emptyset$ reaction on different networks 63

Symbols

a_{ij} .... Adjacency matrix defining the network structure
k .... Degree of a vertex, i.e. the number of edges assigned to a vertex
$P(k)$ .... Degree distribution, probability to select a random vertex with degree k
$P_\mathrm{e}(k)$ .... Edge end distribution, each edge is assembled by two edge ends which root in a vertex of degree k
$P(j,k)$ .... Joint degree distribution, probability to draw a random edge which connects vertices of degree j and degree k
$f(j,k)$ .... Two-point correlation function defined as ratio between the joint degree distribution and the corresponding uncorrelated joint degree distribution
$k_\mathrm{nn}(k)$ .... Average nearest neighbor function, mean degree in the direct neighborhood of a vertex with degree k
r .... Newman factor measuring the strength of two-point correlations
$c(k)$ .... Degree dependent clustering measuring the triangle density for vertices of degree k
α .... Correlation parameter, controls strength of two-point correlations

1 Introduction

Motivation Networks have become an integral part of almost all areas of today's modern societies. With the growing dependence of our very being on networks, the need to maintain them is a vital task for ourselves. One of the most obvious and prominent examples is the Internet [Albert et al., 1999, Barabási & Albert, 1999, Pastor-Satorras & Vespignani, 2004]. It is designed to maintain functioning under attacks against participating computers. Cohen et al. [2000] have shown that a failure of almost all computers is necessary to disintegrate the Internet in case these are attacked by random targeting. If, on the other hand, these attacks are targeted against the most important computers, those which have the most connections, a fraction of only a few percent is sufficient to disintegrate the Internet, revealing the Achilles heel of empirical networks. The current bank crisis demonstrates the devastating consequences to the financial contacts network if major banks fail or abandon contacts towards others due to distrust. This fragility and robustness emerges simultaneously from the topology of networks, which is captured by statistical measures of the network structure. Defining a network as a set of nodes with connections among these nodes, then every node in the network has a distinct number of connections it is assigned to. This number is called the degree k of a node and is statistically described by the degree distribution $P(k)$. This distribution gives the probability to draw a random node from a network with a particular degree k. Analytically, it turns out that the fraction of nodes required to disintegrate a network under random attacks, scales with the second moment of the degree distribution. In the case of the Internet, the functional form of the degree distribution $P(k)$ follows a power-law, $P(k) \propto k^{-\gamma}$, with a scaling exponent γ in the range of $2-3$, meaning a diverging second moment. Networks with a degree distribution following a power-law are termed 'scale-free networks'. In recent years, networks have become a general concept across many scientific fields to model relationships among entities. To the very surprise, most of these networks share the scale-free property. Networks as different as social networks like the collaboration networks of scientists or actors, technological networks such as power grids, Internet and transportation networks, and even biological systems such as protein interaction patterns [Albert & Barabási, 2002, Newman, 2003b] fall into the category of scale-free networks. Along with the ever increasing size and number of networks identified, the need to understand the

1 Introduction

topology of networks is becoming indispensable. Nevertheless, in general a network has to fulfill some function as it serves as a host for some dynamics taking place on the network. The inter-relationship of the topology of a network and a dynamical process taking place on it, which only rather recently became the focus of scientific interest, is the guiding question of this Thesis.

Complex Networks The striking importance of a particular topology of a physical system manifests in the existence of critical exponents, grouping vastly different physical systems into universality classes. These depend in general on the dimensionality, symmetries and very few further system properties. The idea of a network dramatically enhances the classical concept of topologies found in physics. Regular lattices and even fractal topologies can naturally be mapped onto a network. However, the concept of a network is much more general and can even produce complex dynamics solely due to its topology. A fundamentally new feature especially of scale-free networks is the absence of a characteristic scale for the degree of each node. Another remarkable property, inherent to many empirical networks, is the small-world characteristic [Watts & Strogatz, 1998]. It refers to the fact that the average distance from any node to any other node in a network scales as $\ln N$, with N being the number of nodes in the network. In the case of scale-free networks with a scaling exponent $\gamma < 3$, Cohen & Havlin [2003] even proved a scaling of the average node to node distance of $\ln \ln N$.

Altogether, the concept of networks includes complex topologies which display fundamentally new features. As these features emerge from the interplay of many simple entities, a fingerprint of complex behavior, the term complex networks has formed. The strong consequences of complex network topologies for dynamics taking place on such a complex network are subject to current research [Albert & Barabási, 2002, Dorogovtsev & Mendes, 2002, Newman, 2003b].

One of the first analytical results was obtained for dynamics on a network with an arbitrary degree distribution for the much celebrated Ising model [Dorogovtsev et al., 2002, 2005b]. The major observation is a diverging critical magnetization temperature T_c if the second moment of the degree distribution diverges. This divergent second moment of the degree distribution causes a strong heterogeneity in the distribution of degrees and seems to be the cause for many features of complex networks. It is as well the reason for the absence of an epidemic threshold in case of disease spreading [Ahn et al., 2006, Boguñá et al., 2003, Boguñá et al., 2003, Gross et al., 2006], which means that a disease will always persist on a scale-free network. Many further examples of the strong impact by the degree distribution of a complex network on dynamical processes are known to date [Gomez-Gardenes et al., 2007a,b, Newman, 2003b, Nowak et al., 2004, Watts & Strogatz, 1998].

Current Research In 1999 Barabási & Albert studied the topology of the Internet and observed the power-law form of its degree distribution, forming the term 'scale-free network'. Along with this observation, the authors proposed the famous mechanism of preferential attachment as an explanation for the scale-free network topology. The mechanism is based on the idea that a network is constantly growing such that new nodes are added to the existing network by preferentially linking to existing nodes with a high degree in each time-step. Analytical results by Dorogovtsev et al. [2001] prove that the resulting degree distribution is stationary and has a power-law form with a scaling exponent $\gamma = 3$. Barabási & Albert were not the first to discover this basic principle of preferential attachment published in 1999. Yule [1925] introduced this concept already in much earlier. Even though, Barabási & Albert triggered an avalanche of following papers. Initially, the scientific community focused on a better description of networks, resulting in a much improved characterization of large-scale networks. The new observables introduced unraveled many abnormalities of empirical networks in comparison to random networks. Besides the degree distribution and the small-world feature, empirical networks display two-point degree-degree correlations [Newman, 2002], and have a high density of triangles [Newman, 2003a] which are loops of length 3. The two-point degree-degree correlations are defined by the edges of a network which associate vertices of different degrees. While many empirical networks share the scale-free property, two-point correlations are capable to group networks into distinct classes [Newman, 2003b]. For example, most biological networks have negative two-point correlations, technological networks are almost free of two-point correlations, and social networks usually display a strong positive two-point correlation structure. This categorization is an unexplained fact up to date. Apart from correlations Song et al. [2005] were able to apply renormalization to networks, showing that some networks have a fractal topology.

With the increasing knowledge about the topology of networks and the definition of topological measures, the interest in the impact of these mostly statistical measures on dynamics on networks increased. So far analytical results are almost exclusively available for the case of an uncorrelated network topology, which is a first step. Numerical methods are used far more frequent in the literature. However, as the field of complex networks is a very young discipline, there are no common standards yet and some results assumed to be correct at publication time turned out to have flaws. A major source of shortcomings roots in the loose definition of a scale-free network. Many publications use some variant of the preferential attachment scheme proposed by Barabási & Albert to investigate the effects of a scale-free degree distribution on some dynamics. This class of network is referred to in the literature as Barabási-Albert networks and has for a long time been the defacto stan-

1 Introduction

dard network for the investigation of scale-free networks. A closer look at this class of networks reveals that preferential attachment produces very particular networks with very specific topological features, having non-trivial side-effects. An alternative construction scheme for networks is the configuration model. It is based on the idea to construct a network from a random degree sequence following a desired degree distribution [Bollobas, 1980, Molloy & Reed, 1995]. This method is limited to generate uncorrelated networks and even though it seems very obvious to implement, it is rather involved to generate uncorrelated networks correctly, especially in the most interesting case of scale-free networks. The problem of intrinsic degree correlations arises if one does not limit the maximal degree in the degree distribution one wants to attain within the finite network to construct.

Studied Questions The central question of this Thesis is the influence of a complex network topology on a dynamical process on such a network. In general, empirical networks have to fulfill functions, realized by some dynamics running on the network. Assuming that these networks have evolved over time into their current state while optimizing their topology with respect to their function, it is important to note that the dynamical process also influences the topology of a network. To shed light on this general inter-relationship, it is, as a first step, necessary to understand in detail a dynamical process running on a network. In view of the special features scale-free networks exhibit and their frequent observation in empirical networks, it is apparent to study this class of networks. As two-point correlations are very important for empirical networks and even seem to be a general measure to categorize them, I systematically investigated the influence of two-point correlations on the dynamical processes. While these investigations are performed to some extent analytically for uncorrelated networks, I have done these with the help of numerical simulations in the case of correlated networks. There was no reliable method available to systematically study the influence of two-point correlated scale-free networks in a controlled manner. To do so, I introduced an analytical framework along with an algorithm to generate such two-point correlated networks, which was required as an initial step. To study further the influence of dynamics on a topology, I performed as a second step an evolution with respect to a suitable fitness criteria bound to some aspects of the dynamics.

The first dynamical system investigated here belongs to the class of reaction-diffusion processes. These have a stochastic and a deterministic part, capturing the principle characteristics of a large class of dynamically equivalent processes. In particular the diffusion-annihilation process of two species has been studied. It is described by the stoichometric reaction equation $A + B \rightarrow \emptyset$. A second dynamical process from game theory, the Prisoner's Dilemma game, is examined. This dynamical process is ruled by much stronger deterministic mechanisms. Besides, it captures the fascinating question of how cooperation can sustain in a society. As this dynamical process is known to have a property similar to frustration in Ising spin systems of antiferromagnets, the influence of the triangle density is considered as well for this process.

Thesis Outline This Thesis is organized in three major chapters. Every chapter starts with a short overview and ends with a conclusion, summarizing the results obtained.

The following chapter introduces the analytical description of networks, including observables used to measure topological properties. The subsequent section presents the analytical framework along with a short description of the algorithms used to generate the networks for the numerical investigations. These include a methodology to generate two-point correlated networks which is already published by us, Weber & Porto [2007], and further work by Andreas Pusch, who collaborated with me as a diploma student and developed an algorithm to control the triangle density within a network on top of two-point correlations, appeared as Pusch et al. [2008a]. This is followed by a thorough discussion of finite networks, since finite-size effects are of great importance for the study of scale-free networks.

The next chapter presents the dynamical processes studied here, a reaction-diffusion and the Prisoner's Dilemma. The major results for the diffusion-annihilation process concerning the analytical part on uncorrelated networks [Weber & Porto, 2006], and regarding the numerical analysis of two-point correlations [Weber et al., 2008], are already published in the literature. The findings about the cumulative payoff version of the Prisoner's Dilemma game were worked out by Andreas Pusch in collaboration with me and are likewise published by Pusch et al. [2008b]. A publication concerning the efficiency ruled Prisoner's Dilemma is currently in preparation [Weber & Porto, 2009a].

The subsequent chapter treats the question, how dynamics interact with a topology. Performing this in the framework of evolution, network mutation schemes and fitness measures are introduced as a first step. The results regarding the network mutation schemes are arranged for a publication in the near future [Weber & Porto, 2009b]. Consequently, the mutation schemes are applied to an evolution of the two dynamical processes considered here.

The Thesis closes with an overall conclusion and discussion. The Appendix covers details about analytical derivations, the numerical algorithms used to generate the networks and the simulation schemes of the dynamical processes.

2 Structure of Complex Networks

In mathematics graph theory describes the structure and properties of networks. Within this framework, graphs are defined as a set of vertices and a set of edges. Each edge connects two vertices and may be directed or undirected, depending on the type of graph. The seminal work in this field by Erdős & Rényi [Erdős & Rényi, 1959, 1960, 1961] concentrated on graphs which are random in the sense that two vertices were connected by an edge with a certain probability p, resulting in graphs with a Poissonian degree distribution. Since then, many further models of random graphs have been proposed [Barabási & Albert, 1999, Dorogovtsev & Mendes, 2002, Watts & Strogatz, 1998, Xulvi-Brunet & Sokolov, 2004].

This Thesis focuses on networks with a scale-free degree distribution with controlled two-point correlations. If applicable, the density of triangles is being adjusted as well. In view of the dynamics to perform, these networks must fulfill a few physical requirements such that they are undirected (i), do not have neither any multiple connections among two distinct vertices (ii) nor any self-connections (iii) and have to consist of only one connected component (iv).

Within the first section, an analytical description of networks is introduced along with measures used in this Thesis which statistically describe large-scale networks. The subsequent section provides the theoretical framework along with the principle ideas behind the algorithms used to generate the networks within the numerical simulations. This is followed by a discussion of finite-size effects which are very important in the context of scale-free networks. Numerical simulations and every empirical network are affected by their inherent finite size, limiting every power-law degree distribution to some cut-off scale.

2.1 Network Description

An undirected network consisting of N nodes or vertices is defined by its $N \times N$ adjacency matrix a_{ij}. Requiring the absence of multiple- and self-connections, this

2 Structure of Complex Networks

matrix is a traceless, symmetric matrix and defined by

$$a_{ij} = \begin{cases} 1 & \text{vertex } i \text{ is connected to vertex } j \\ 0 & \text{otherwise} \end{cases}. \quad (2.1)$$

Statistical observables concerning the topology of networks and some of their most important properties used throughout this Thesis are presented below.

Degree k. The number of edges leaving a vertex is called its degree k.

Degree distribution $P(k)$. The distribution of all degrees found in a network is termed the degree distribution $P(k)$. It represents the probability to select a random vertex with a given degree k. Averages calculated with respect to the degree distribution $P(k)$ will be noted by $\overline{\cdot}$ such that the mean degree of a network is given by $\overline{k} = \sum_k k\, P(k)$.

Edge end distribution $P_e(k)$. Each edge in a network can be thought of being assembled by two edge ends which are themselves assigned to distinct vertices. Drawing an edge end is equivalent to randomly select an edge and then select at random one of the two vertices which are connected by the drawn edge. A vertex of degree k therefore has exactly k edge ends connected to it. From this it follows that the degree distribution $P(k)$ and the edge end distribution $P_e(k)$ are related such that

$$P_e(k) = P(k) \frac{k}{\overline{k}}. \quad (2.2)$$

Averages with respect to the edge end distribution $P_e(k)$ are denoted by $\langle \cdot \rangle$ and have to be carefully distinguished from former averages with respect to the degree distribution.

Joint degree distribution $P(j,k)$. Two-point correlations are statistically encoded by the joint degree distribution $P(j,k)$. It measures the probability to draw a random edge from a network with edge ends of degree j and degree k simultaneously. Important properties are the symmetry under arguments exchange, $P(j,k) = P(k,j)$, and the relation

$$P_e(k) = \sum_j P(j,k) \quad (2.3)$$

to the edge end distribution. In the special case of no correlations, the joint degree distribution $P_{uc}(j,k)$ function factorizes into a product of the edge end distributions

$$P_{uc}(j,k) \equiv P_e(j)\, P_e(k). \quad (2.4)$$

8

Closely related to the joint degree distribution is the conditional degree distribution $P(j|k)$ which is derived straightforward from the joint degree distribution,

$$P(j|k) = \frac{P(j,k)}{P_{\text{e}}(k)}. \tag{2.5}$$

Two-point correlation function $f(j,k)$**.** A convenient, alternative representation of two-point correlations is given by the correlation function [Song et al., 2006]

$$f(j,k) \equiv \frac{P(j,k)}{P_{\text{uc}}(j,k)}, \tag{2.6}$$

relating the joint degree distribution to the uncorrelated case. Values different from 1 indicate the presence of two-point correlations.

Average nearest neighbor degree $k_{\text{nn}}(k)$**.** The last two measures are rather complex functional objects and not very intuitive. A coarse-grained view is given by the average nearest neighbor function

$$k_{\text{nn}}(k) \equiv \sum_{j} j\, P(j|k). \tag{2.7}$$

This function represents the average degree a vertex with fixed degree k has in its neighborhood. An interesting property to note is the relation arising from averaging Eq. (2.7) with respect to $P_{\text{e}}(k)$,

$$\langle k_{\text{nn}}(k) \rangle = \langle k \rangle, \tag{2.8}$$

which is a generally valid relation. A network is said to have (dis-)assortative two-point correlations if the average nearest neighbor function $k_{\text{nn}}(k)$ is a monotonously (de-)increasing function.

Newman factor r**.** Newman [Newman, 2002] found a way to quantify the overall two-point correlations in a network with a scalar value. The Newman factor

$$r \equiv \frac{1}{\sigma_e^2} \sum_{j,k} jk\, [P(j,k) - P_{\text{e}}(j)\, P_{\text{e}}(k)] \tag{2.9}$$

is the Pearson correlation coefficient of degrees from vertices connected by edges. The Newman factor is normalized to fall in the range of $[-1, 1]$. A positive (negative) value corresponds to an (dis-)assortative two-point correlation structure.

2 Structure of Complex Networks

Clustering c. A general treatment of three-point correlations is rather involved. Instead, it is common to concentrate on triangles which are a special form of three-point correlations. A triangle is made up of 3 vertices which are mutually connected to form a loop. Clustering refers to this special form of loop. The clustering coefficient

$$c_i \equiv \frac{2T_i}{k_i(k_i - 1)} \tag{2.10}$$

for vertex i was originally defined by Watts & Strogatz [1998]. Here, T_i denotes the number of triangles passing through vertex i which is normalized to the maximal number of possible triangles. It is common use to average this quantity over the set $\mathcal{V}(k)$ of vertices with the same degree k, yielding the degree dependent clustering coefficient

$$c(k) \equiv \frac{2}{k(k-1)P(k)N} \sum_{i \in \mathcal{V}(k)} T_i. \tag{2.11}$$

2.2 Randomized Networks

This Thesis concentrates on scale-free networks which have a power-law degree distribution

$$P(k) \propto k^{-\gamma} \tag{2.12}$$

and are random with respect to all other properties besides two-point correlations and clustering which are controlled by tunable parameters.

Random networks consist in general out of multiple components which are disconnected and of varying size. If the degree distribution fulfills the condition

$$\overline{k^2} - 2\overline{k} > 0 \Leftrightarrow \frac{\overline{k^2}}{2\overline{k}} > 1, \tag{2.13}$$

a largest component forms [Molloy & Reed, 1995]. The largest component scales with the system size N and contains usually the major fraction of nodes within a network. For the case of scale-free networks the condition (2.13) translates into

$$\frac{\overline{k^2}}{2\overline{k}} = \frac{1}{2}\left|\frac{\gamma - 2}{\gamma - 3}\right| \times \begin{cases} N & 1 < \gamma < 2 \\ k_{\min}^{\gamma-2} N^{3-\gamma} & 2 < \gamma < 3 \\ k_{\min} & \gamma > 3 \end{cases}. \tag{2.14}$$

Throughout this Thesis the scaling parameter γ has been set within the range $[2, 4]$, motivated by real-world networks. To ensure that the largest component always spans almost the whole network, the minimal degree $k_{\min}$ is set to 2 in all numerical simulations.

2.2.1 Uncorrelated Networks

This class of networks is widely used for analytical calculations as it allows for many simplifications within analytics. The key property of an uncorrelated network is the product form of the joint degree distribution

$$P(j,k) = P_{\text{uc}}(j,k) = P_{\text{e}}(j)\,P_{\text{e}}(k). \tag{2.15}$$

As a consequence, the average nearest neighbor function $k_{\text{nn}}(k)$ becomes independent of k (by Eq. (2.8) equal to $\langle k \rangle$) and the Newman factor r vanishes. The configuration model (CM) [Bollobás, 1980, Molloy & Reed, 1998] is the standard algorithm to generate networks with a fixed degree distribution. The idea is to construct a network from an *a priori* given degree sequence which is drawn from the desired degree distribution $P(k)$. This degree sequence is then transformed into a discrete representation of the edge end distribution $P_{\text{e}}(k)$. Edges are formed by drawing two edge ends from this set which are subsequently joined to connect the respective vertices. Consecutively, the two edge ends are removed from the set. Since the two draws of edge ends are independent, the resulting probability of a connection being formed is exactly equal to $P_{\text{e}}(k)\,P_{\text{e}}(j)$. However, due to the restriction of a simple graph, meaning the absence of self- and multiple-connections, some of the sampled edges have to be neglected, causing intrinsic degree correlations to arise. These intrinsic correlations emerge in particular in the case of scale-free networks as they are bound to finite-size effects due to the maximal degree k_{max} in a finite scale-free network. The choice of the maximal degree k_{max} turns out to be quite peculiar in the generation of a scale-free network [Catanzaro *et al.*, 2005b]. Generated networks become two-point correlated in an uncontrolled manner if the scaling of the maximal degree k_{max} with the system size N is inappropriate. This makes an in-depth treatment of finite-size effects necessary as presented in Sec. 2.3.

2.2.2 Two-Point Correlated Networks

In contrast to uncorrelated networks, two-point correlated networks have a joint degree distribution deviating from the simple product form. An algorithm to generate networks numerically with an *a priori* fixed joint degree distribution $P(j,k)$ and being random in respect to all other properties has been introduced by myself [Weber & Porto, 2007]. The idea is to draw edges in a two-step sampling scheme. The joint degree distribution fixes subsequent distributions ($P(j|k)$, $P_{\text{e}}(k)$, and $P(k)$), such that some considerations, which are discussed below, have to be made in order to specify *a priori* a scale-free degree distribution besides two-point correlations. In analogy to the CM algorithm, an edge end is drawn at first with respect to the

2 Structure of Complex Networks

corresponding edge end distribution $P_{\rm e}(k)$ while the second edge end is drawn with weights according to the conditional degree distribution $P(j|k)$. This results in a distribution of edges according to $P_{\rm e}(k)\,P(j|k)$ which is exactly equal to the joint degree distribution $P(j,k)$. The major challenges for a numerical implementation are the strong discretization effects and the extremely small probabilities which arise especially in the case of scale-free networks. A detailed description of the algorithm, which solves these problems, can be found in Appendix A.2.1. The algorithm generates networks of arbitrary joint degree distribution $P(j,k)$ with very high accuracy and efficiency.

Controlling two-point correlations in a network while fixing the degree distribution to a particular functional form has strong implications for the joint degree distribution $P(j,k)$ or equivalently for the correlation function $f(j,k)$. A formalism to allow the two-point correlations to be tuned by some parameter with an *a priori* fixed degree distribution $P(k)$ is required.

In a first step, inter-relationships among the introduced quantities from Sec. 2.1 are calculated. These help to find an adequate control parameter for the two-point correlations. From the definition of the Newman factor (2.9) the relation to the correlation function (2.6) follows directly to be

$$r\sigma_{\rm e}^2 = \langle jk\,(f(j,k) - 1)\rangle_{j,k} = \langle jk\,f(j,k)\rangle_{j,k} - \langle k\rangle^2\,. \tag{2.16}$$

By the notation $\langle \cdot \rangle_{j,k}$ the average with respect to $P_{\rm e}(k)$ is to be taken over the indices j and k simultaneously. The correlation function $f(j,k)$ is also tightly connected to the average nearest neighbor function $k_{\rm nn}(k)$. Using that the conditional probability $P(j|k)$ is equal to $P(j,k)/P_{\rm e}(k) = P_{\rm e}(j)\,f(j,k)$, the definition of Eq. (2.7) turns into

$$k_{\rm nn}(k) = \langle j\,f(j,k)\rangle_j\,. \tag{2.17}$$

Multiplying the average nearest neighbor function $k_{\rm nn}(k)$ with $k\,P_{\rm e}(k)$ and summing over all k, results in

$$\langle k\,k_{\rm nn}(k)\rangle = \langle jk\,f(j,k)\rangle_{j,k}\,, \tag{2.18}$$

which yields, substituted into Eq. (2.16),

$$r\sigma_{\rm e}^2 = \langle k\,k_{\rm nn}(k)\rangle - \langle k\rangle^2\,. \tag{2.19}$$

From the constraint of a given degree distribution $P(k)$ it follows that an integration over either argument of the joint degree distribution $P(j,k)$ has to be equal to the corresponding edge end distribution $P_{\rm e}(j)$ (or $P_{\rm e}(k)$). Thus, the correlation function $f(j,k)$ has to fulfill the condition,

$$P_{\rm e}(k) = \sum_j P(j,k) = P_{\rm e}(k)\,\langle f(j,k)\rangle_j\,, \tag{2.20}$$

2.2 Randomized Networks

which means
$$\langle f(j,k)\rangle_j = 1 \, . \tag{2.21}$$
The considerations so far are general. To control two-point correlations within the network, an explicit correlation function $f(j,k)$ is needed, which has the property of Eq. (2.21), and produces a joint degree distribution which has a given average nearest neighbor function $k_{\mathrm{nn}}(k)$. A simple ansatz for the correlation function is
$$f(j,k) = 1 + h(j)\,h(k) \, . \tag{2.22}$$
This functional form may be understood as a series expansion of first order, fulfilling the necessary symmetry property that the correlation function is constant under exchange of indices j and k. Plugging this ansatz into Eq. (2.17) produces
$$k_{\mathrm{nn}}(k) = \langle k\rangle + \langle j\,h(j)\rangle\,h(k) \, , \tag{2.23}$$
which means that
$$h(k) = \frac{k_{\mathrm{nn}}(k) - \langle k\rangle}{\langle j\,h(j)\rangle} \, . \tag{2.24}$$
The constant $\langle j\,h(j)\rangle$ can easily be calculated by multiplying Eq. (2.24) with $k\,P_{\mathrm{e}}(k)$ and summing over all k. Rearranging the terms then yields
$$\langle k\,h(k)\rangle = \sqrt{\langle k\,k_{\mathrm{nn}}(k)\rangle - \langle k\rangle^2} = \sqrt{r\sigma_{\mathrm{e}}^2} \, . \tag{2.25}$$
Finally, the correlation function $f(j,k)$ has the form
$$f(j,k) = 1 + \frac{1}{r}\frac{(k_{\mathrm{nn}}(j) - \langle k\rangle)\,(k_{\mathrm{nn}}(k) - \langle k\rangle)}{\sigma_{\mathrm{e}}^2} \, . \tag{2.26}$$
Employing condition (2.21) to the ansatz in Eq. (2.22) gives
$$\langle h(j)\rangle = 0 \, . \tag{2.27}$$
This property is consistent with the functional form of $h(k)$ in Eq. (2.24), since the average of $h(k)$ over k with respect to the edge end distribution $P_{\mathrm{e}}(k)$ yields zero by usage of Eq. (2.8) ($\langle k_{\mathrm{nn}}(k)\rangle = \langle k\rangle$). Furthermore, Eq. (2.8) helps to construct valid average nearest neighbor functions $k_{\mathrm{nn}}(k)$ with an arbitrary functional dependence on the degree k. Taking a sufficiently smooth and positive weighting function $g(k)$, the corresponding $k_{\mathrm{nn}}(k)$ compatible with Eq. (2.8) is then
$$k_{\mathrm{nn}}(k) = \frac{\langle k\rangle}{\langle g(k)\rangle}\,g(k) \, . \tag{2.28}$$
However, the resulting correlation function $f(j,k)$ is still constrained by even further conditions [Boguñá et al., 2004, Dorogovtsev et al., 2005a, Lee et al., 2006].

2 Structure of Complex Networks

For example, the ratio $r_{j,k}$ as introduced by Boguñá et al. [2004] is defined as the actual number of connections $E_{j,k}$ ($= P(j,k)\bar{k}N$) divided by the maximal number of connections $m_{j,k}$ among the degree classes j and k. For networks without multiple edges this ratio is given by

$$r_{j,k} = \frac{E_{j,k}}{m_{j,k}} = \frac{P(j,k)}{\min\{P_e(j), P_e(k), \bar{k}N \, P_e(j)P_e(k)/jk\}}. \qquad (2.29)$$

This ratio must always be in the range between 0 and 1 for all valid degree classes j and k present in the network,

$$0 \leq r_{j,k} \leq 1 \; \forall \, j,k \in [k_{\min}, k_{\max}]. \qquad (2.30)$$

From this condition the admissible degree range $[k_{\min}, k_{\max}]$ becomes dependent on the details of the correlation function $f(j,k)$. An average nearest neighbor function $k_{\mathrm{nn}}(k)$ suitable to easily tune two-point correlations and being compatible with the above requirements, turns out to be

$$k_{\mathrm{nn}}(k) \propto \exp\left[\ln^\alpha\left(1 + \frac{k}{k_{\min}}\right)\right]. \qquad (2.31)$$

This functional form introduces the two-point correlation parameter α, making the strength of two-point correlations tunable with a single scalar. A value of $\alpha = 0$ corresponds to an uncorrelated two-point correlation structure while $\alpha > 0$ ($\alpha < 0$) will result in (dis-)assortative network topologies.

2.2.3 Two-Point Correlated Networks with Clustering

The triangle densities within many empirical networks have been found to be much larger than one would expect from random graph theory. Interestingly, Dorogovtsev [2004] proved that clustering within random networks with a prescribed joint degree distribution $P(j,k)$ is a finite-size effect, disappearing in the thermodynamic limit. Nevertheless, triangles are still important due to their relevance in empirical networks. Since clustering is a special form of three-point correlations, it is ruled by the two-point correlation structure of a network. This has been pointed out by Serrano & Boguñá [2005], who published an algorithm being capable to generate uncorrelated networks with a prescribed degree distribution and tunable degree dependent clustering. Building on these ideas, the diploma student Andreas Pusch implemented an enhanced algorithm in collaboration with me, allowing to fix *a priori* the two-point correlations by the joint degree distribution $P(j,k)$ and the degree dependent clustering $c(k)$. The rather involved algorithm is presented in Appendix A.2.2.

Analytical calculations from Serrano & Boguñá show that the density of triangles is limited by the joint degree distribution $P(j,k)$ of a network, resulting in an upper limit $\lambda(k)$ for the degree dependent clustering function $c(k)$. Since an edge which connects vertices i and j with respective degrees k_i and k_j cannot be part of more triangles than $\min(k_i, k_j) - 1$, the number of triangles is constrained for any vertex i in the network by

$$T_i \leq \sum_j a_{ij}[\min(k_i, k_j) - 1]. \qquad (2.32)$$

From this, the upper limit $\lambda(k)$ is obtained by averaging Eq. (2.32) over vertices of the same degree k, which yields

$$\lambda(k) = 1 - \frac{1}{k-1} \sum_{j=1}^{k}(k-j) P(j|k) \geq c(k). \qquad (2.33)$$

This function always decreases with increasing values of k and is strongly dependent on the functional form of the average nearest neighbor function $k_{\text{nn}}(k)$. With this upper bound $\lambda(k)$, the degree dependent clustering $c(k)$ can be rewritten in terms of an effective degree dependent clustering $c_{\text{eff}}(k)$,

$$c(k) = c_{\text{eff}}(k)\, \lambda(k). \qquad (2.34)$$

The range of $c_{\text{eff}}(k)$ is bound to the interval $[0,1]$. For simplicity, only clustered networks with a constant effective degree independent clustering

$$c_{\text{eff}}(k) = \mu \qquad (2.35)$$

are considered in this Thesis.

2.3 Finite Scale-Free Networks

Analytical results on the impact of an arbitrary degree distribution, with special focus on a scale-free degree distribution, on some dynamical process on such a network are commonly calculated in the thermodynamical limit ($N \to \infty$). In addition, it is common use to assume some network ensemble on which the results are valid. This discards the effects of discretization and finite-size, two major effects every finite network is subject to.

To illustrate how strongly these two issues affect finite scale-free distributions, Fig. 2.1 shows the frequency distribution of a sample with size $N = 10^4$ which was drawn in respect to a scale-free degree distribution with a scaling exponent of $\gamma = 2.5$. The frequency distribution is, in contrast to the degree distribution, not

2 Structure of Complex Networks

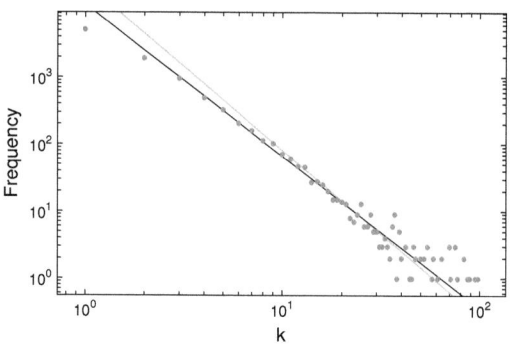

Figure 2.1: Sampled frequency distribution of a scale-free distribution with scaling exponent $\gamma = 2.5$.

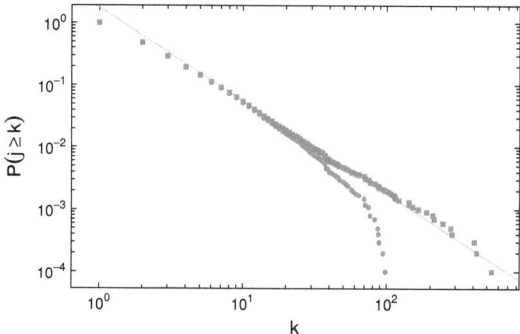

Figure 2.2: Cumulative degree distribution of a sampled scale-free distribution with a scaling exponent $\gamma = 2.5$ without limiting the maximal degree $k_{\max}$ (square) and with a maximal degree of $k_{\max} = 10^2$ (circle).

normalized to the total number of vertices N and is also referred to as a histogram. If normalized and for infinite system size, the degree distribution and the frequency distribution become equal. For finite systems, the minimal probability for the degree distribution is $1/N$ while the minimal frequency is 1, making the latter better suited to represent a single sample. The discretization effects are most visible for large degrees k, since the minimal frequency is 1. However, by comparing to the reference line with a slope of -2.5 in light gray, the deviations for small degrees k are apparent as well. These discretization effects are introduced by the fact that degrees are always integer numbers. It should be stressed that much of the literature uses such a frequency plot to estimate the scaling parameter of an empirical network. A least squares fit, also shown in Fig. 2.1 as solid black line, underestimates the scaling parameter. This point has recently been brought up by Li et al. [2006]. Li et al. emphasize the importance of using a cumulative density distribution (CDD), presented in Fig. 2.2,

$$P(j \geq k) = \sum_{k'=k}^{\infty} P(k'). \tag{2.36}$$

The CDD does not suffer from most of the problems a frequency distribution is inherently bound to. An estimation of the scaling parameter using the CDD is much more reliable for various reasons. It is much more robust with respect to variability and has the major advantage that no binning is necessary, a common source of many mistakes. The light gray reference line in Fig. 2.2 demonstrates these advantages as the observed discretization effects are much less apparent. However, the sample shown by squares has been drawn without a restriction on the largest possible degree $k_{\max}$. This is, for various reasons, not applicable for the numerical generation of scale-free networks with defined two-point correlations as explained below. Limiting the range of drawn degrees within the sample to values lower than 10^2 (circle), reveals an exponential cut-off in the CDD which is apparently bound to any finite system and can be observed for the sample with no upper limit (square) as well, only much weaker. These considerations underline the use of large ensembles and careful inspection of results with respect to variability.

Since the realization probability for large degrees k decreases quite rapidly even for a scale-free degree distribution, it is necessary to limit the maximal degree $k_{\max}$ within a finite network ensemble to prevent large fluctuations within the realized degree sequences. Cohen et al. [2000] introduced such so-called natural cut-off

$$k_{\max}^{\text{natural}} \propto N^{1/(\gamma-1)}, \tag{2.37}$$

which is defined by the condition that the CDD of the scale-free degree distribution is equal to $1/N$. It is important to emphasize that this cut-off is by no means induced by the topology of the complex network.

2 Structure of Complex Networks

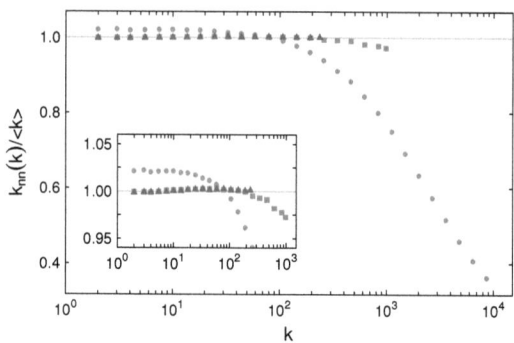

Figure 2.3: Normalized average nearest neighbor function $k_{nn}(k)/\langle k \rangle$ for an uncorrelated scale-free graph with a scaling exponent $\gamma = 2.5$ and the maximal degrees k_{max} equals to $k_{max}^{natural}$ (circle), $k_{max}^{structural}$ (square), and $k_{max}^{ensemble}$ (triangle). The size of the graph is $N = 10^6$ and the inset shows the data for degrees $k < 10^3$ to increase sensitivity against the expected value of 1 which is marked by a reference line.

Generating an uncorrelated scale-free network with such a cut-off for the maximal degree k should yield an average nearest neighbor function which is for all degrees k exactly equals to $\langle k \rangle$. Figure 2.3 shows the resulting average nearest neighbor function $k_{nn}(k)$ normalized to $\langle k \rangle$ for a scale-free network of size $N = 10^6$ with a scaling exponent $\gamma = 2.5$ for different values of the maximal degree k_{max}. The normalization is necessary to suitably compare the different average nearest neighbor functions $k_{nn}(k)$ since the constant $\langle k \rangle$ is dependent on the maximal degree k_{max}. The natural cut-off is indicated by circles and reveals disassortativity within the network which is confirmed by the Newman factor $r = -0.01$. It turns out that in this regime of the scaling exponent γ, the natural cut-off is not compatible with the condition of Eq. (2.30). The Eq. (2.30) can easily be used to determine the so-called structural cut-off. In the case of scale-free networks, Eq. (2.29) reduces for sufficiently large degrees j and k to $r_{j,k} = jk\,f(j,k)/\overline{k}N$ and therefore defines a maximal degree k_{max} at the upper bound for the ratio ($r_{k_{max},k_{max}} = 1$). With this criterion, one obtains, in the case of uncorrelated networks having a constant correlation function $f(j,k) = 1$, the scale-parameter independent cut-off

$$k_{max}^{structural} \propto N^{1/2}. \qquad (2.38)$$

This is smaller than the natural cut-off for values of the scale-parameter in the range $2 < \gamma \leq 3$. The result of applying this maximal degree in the example chosen above is shown in Fig. 2.3, denoted by square symbols. While the difference to unity is much improved in comparison to the former natural cut-off, the normalized average nearest neighbor function $k_{\text{nn}}(k)/\langle k \rangle$ still falls slightly below unity for large degrees. Newer calculations by Dorogovtsev et al. [2005a] reveal that this structural cut-off is still too large in that particular range of the scale-parameter γ and causes intrinsic correlations to arise within otherwise uncorrelated networks without self- or multiple-edges. Due to the maximal degree k_{max} being too large and the required constraints, the vertices with large degrees k do have a tendency to connect preferentially with low degree vertices which effectively yields unwanted disassortativity. The reason for the failure of condition (2.30) in the case of scale-free networks with a scale-parameter γ in the range $(2,3]$ can be seen in the strong fluctuations in the degree distribution as only the first moment of the degree distribution $P(k)$ is finite.

The approach taken by Dorogovtsev et al. is based on a statistical ensemble ansatz. A canonical network ensemble is defined as the set of networks with a fixed set of vertices and a fixed number of edges. The final networks are then the out-come of an evolution process in which randomly chosen edges are removed and simultaneously added to pairs of vertices in the network. Each pair of vertices is chosen at random with weights given by the product of a preferential function $f(j)f(k)$ where j and k are the degrees of the respective vertices. With the preferential function $f(k) = k + 1 - \gamma$ and beneath the critical temperature, the authors observe that the degree distribution becomes scale-free. However, depending on the finiteness of the second moment of the degree distribution, Dorogovtsev et al. find different cut-offs of the degree range

$$k_{\text{max}}^{\text{ensemble}} = \begin{cases} N^{1/2} & \text{if } \gamma > 3 \\ N^{1/(5-\gamma)} & \text{if } 2 < \gamma \leq 3. \end{cases} \quad (2.39)$$

The evolution process driving a network into this equilibrium network is, of course, neither the same as constructing a network with the CM algorithm nor any other algorithm used in this Thesis. The used algorithms fix *a priori* both, the number of vertices and the number of edges just like the canonical network ensemble defined by Dorogovtsev et al.. Thus, these algorithms can be interpreted to produce graphs which are members of the canonical network ensemble below the critical temperature, since the algorithms used evidently yield random networks with the correct degree distribution. Consequently, the ensemble maximal degree $k_{\text{max}}^{\text{ensemble}}$ applies equally to the numerically generated networks.

The considerations so far only cover the case of uncorrelated networks. However, networks with a fast increasing average nearest neighbor function $k_{\text{nn}}(k)$, as it can

2 Structure of Complex Networks

arise in assortative networks, are much more sensitive to intrinsic degree correlations than uncorrelated networks. Thus, a maximal degree k_{max} yielding uncorrelated networks can still be too large if used in the context of assortative networks. An assortative network requires that vertices with a large degree are preferably connected to other vertices with a large degree, but it can happen that the vertices with the largest degrees do not have sufficient vertices available with such a large degree due to the interdiction of multiple- and self-edges. The average nearest neighbor function $k_{nn}(k)$, presented in Eq. (2.31), accounts for this by logarithmically damping the increase in $k_{nn}(k)$ with increasing degree k. In effect, the average nearest neighbor function can be used with a maximal degree as identified by [Dorogovtsev et al., 2005a] with the maximal degree $k_{max} = k_{max}^{ensemble}$.

2.4 Conclusion

In summary, this chapter introduced the key measures used in this Thesis to characterize the topology of the studied networks. An analytical framework allowing to tune two-point correlations and clustering has been derived. The two-point correlations are adjustable in the presented ansatz via the average nearest neighbor function $k_{nn}(k)$ which was set to a function tunable by the introduced correlation parameter α. The clustering has been re-expressed with the help of the upper bound $\lambda(k)$ which is fixed by the two-point correlations within the network.

Furthermore, the detailed discussion of finite size effects within scale-free distributions revealed that every finite sample is strongly affected by these. Extremely small realization probabilities, discretization effects and large fluctuations make large ensembles within numerical studies of scale-free networks necessary.

Another important finding is the required scaling of the maximal degree k_{max} with the system size N in order to prevent intrinsic degree correlations to arise.

3 Dynamics on Complex Networks

To answer the question of the inter-relationship between dynamics and topology of a network requires that the particular dynamics studied must fulfill certain integral properties. The dynamics should be well studied on 'classical' topologies, represent a large class of equivalent dynamical processes, and be made up of rather elementary interaction rules which result in complex behavior but still allow for an analytical treatment.

One dynamics studied here belongs to the class of reaction-diffusion dynamics. This class of dynamics features stochasticity due to the diffusion and a deterministic part by the reaction. These primary features are even present in the most elementary form of a diffusion-annihilation process. This process is in particular representative for a generic chemical reaction which is not auto-catalytic and acyclic. This class of system is well studied on lattices and many other special geometries like fractals. Due to the annihilation the density of particles is constantly decreasing. For classical topologies the decrease of the particle density scales generally linear or weaker than linear with time. This is in striking contrast to the behavior observed on scale-free networks which show a super-linear decay for a scaling exponent γ in the range 2 to 3. Furthermore, the studied two-component diffusion-annihilation process $A + B \to \emptyset$ displays patterns on regular lattices, as a segregation of the components occurs, which is much weaker on scale-free networks than on regular lattices. Two-point correlations turn out to influence these patterns and the overall efficiency of the dynamical process.

In addition, the famous Prisoner's Dilemma game is studied. Unrelated individuals (so that there is no kin selection) are allowed to choose among the two strategies cooperation and defection. The dilemma of the game arises from the advantageous defection strategy for an individual within a single interaction while the cooperation strategy would result in an advantage for all individuals in the long-run. In large, well-mixed populations, the dominant strategy is defection. Recent studies [Gomez-Gardenes et al., 2007a] on Barabási-Albert networks, which have a scale-free degree distribution, $\gamma = 3$, and particular further properties due to their construction scheme, revealed a dominance of the cooperation strategy, a behavior previously unobserved. A key property of the Prisoner's Dilemma is the build up of a stationary state. This allows for detailed characterization of the patterns formed.

3 Dynamics on Complex Networks

3.1 Reaction-Diffusion Process

From the class of reaction-diffusion systems, the particular type of diffusion-annihilation dynamics is extremely well studied [Torney & McConnell, 1983, Toussaint & Wilczek, 1983]. The one- and two-component reactions in particular show anomalous behavior in low dimensions. This is caused by pattern formation in the form of the build up of a depletion zone for the former and a segregation of the two components for the latter. The critical dimension is 2 for both dynamics. The derived mean-field (MF) prediction for the continuous particle density decay reveals a power-law relationship in time

$$\frac{1}{\rho} - \frac{1}{\rho_0} \propto t^f, \qquad (3.1)$$

where ρ_0 is the particle density at $t = 0$, and the value of f is 1 above the critical dimension. The value of f below the critical dimension and within different geometries like fractals, is always less than 1. A super-linear decay with $f > 1$ has only been observed on scale-free networks to date. Gallos & Argyrakis were the first to discover this super-linear relationship in numerical simulations [Gallos & Argyrakis, 2004, 2005]. Shortly afterwards these results were backed up by an analytical MF calculation by Catanzaro et al. [2005a] for the case of the one-component $A + A \to \emptyset$ reaction. These calculations showed the dependence of f on the scaling exponent γ in the case of scale-free networks to be

$$f(\gamma) = \begin{cases} \dfrac{1}{\gamma - 2} & 2 < \gamma < 3 \\ 1 & \gamma \geq 3 \end{cases}. \qquad (3.2)$$

The reason for this extremely fast density decay originates in the existence of a small number of vertices with very large degrees (so-called hubs) in a scale-free network. As the $A + A \to \emptyset$ analysis shows, the density is constantly $1/2$ for vertices with a degree $k > k_c = \overline{k}/2\rho(t)$. The two-component reaction $A + B \to \emptyset$, in turn, is much more involved, since a new feature, a 'jamming' effect, is introduced.

The $A + B \to \emptyset$ dynamics is defined on a network to start by random assignment of at most one particle per vertex. A particle on a vertex may diffuse along a randomly selected edge emanating from the hosting vertex to an adjacent vertex. Depending on the state of the adjacent vertex at the other end of that edge, three cases can occur: (i) If the adjacent vertex is empty, the particle moves to the new vertex. (ii) In case a particle of the other species resides at the adjacent vertex, the annihilation takes place and the particle densities are decreased appropriately. (iii) If a particle of the same species is located at the adjacent vertex, the diffusion step is impossible. The third possibility is responsible for the occurrence of jamming and results in an extra term within the differential equation describing the time-evolution of the particle densities. Nevertheless, this term becomes irrelevant in comparison to the other terms within the long-time, low-density limit, as shown below.

3.1.1 Analytical Results

The detailed analytical treatment of the $A + B \to \emptyset$ results can be found in the Appendix A.1 and is already published by us [Weber & Porto, 2006]. A sketch of the derivation and a summary of the major results are presented in the following. An integral assumption of the MF ansatz, motivated by the importance the degree k of each vertex has, is the statistical equivalence of vertices with the same degree k. This is implemented by averaging over the set of vertices $\mathcal{V}(k)$ which have the same degree k, also referred to as degree classes. As a result the overall particle densities $\rho^{(a)}(t)$ and $\rho^{(b)}(t)$ can be obtained by averaging over the densities from all degree classes k,

$$\rho^{(a)}(t) = \sum_k \rho_k^{(a)}(t) \, P(k) = \overline{\rho_k^{(a)}(t)}, \qquad (3.3)$$

where $\rho_k^{(a)}$ ($\rho_k^{(b)}$) is the density of particles of type A (B) which are located on vertices with degree k. Modeling the diffusion as a Poisson process [Kampen, 1992] and assuming the absence of two-point correlations, the resulting differential equation for the degree-resolved densities is

$$\frac{d\rho_k^{(a)}}{dt} = -\rho_k^{(a)} + \frac{k}{\overline{k}}\left[1 - 3\rho_k^{(a)}\right]\rho^{(a)} + \rho_k^{(a)} \langle \rho_k^{(a)} \rangle. \qquad (3.4)$$

For the sake of simplicity, the initial densities have been set equal, $\rho^{(a)}(t=0) = \rho^{(b)}(t=0)$, and the explicit time dependence of the particle densities has been suppressed for improved readability. Due to symmetry, the equivalent equation for $\rho_k^{(b)}$ can be obtained by interchanging indices A and B. The time evolution of the overall density $\rho^{(a)}$ follows straightforwardly by averaging Eq. (3.4) in respect to the degree distribution

$$\frac{d\rho^{(a)}}{dt} = -\rho^{(a)} \langle \rho_k^{(b)} \rangle - \rho^{(b)} \langle \rho_k^{(a)} \rangle. \qquad (3.5)$$

To proceed, a solution for $\rho_k^{(a)}$ is necessary. The differential equation (3.4) is very similar to the one previously found for the $A + A \to \emptyset$ process [Catanzaro et al., 2005a], with an additional term $\rho_k^{(a)} \langle \rho_k^{(a)} \rangle$ and a coefficient of 3 instead of 2 in front of $\rho_k^{(a)}$. The additional term can be shown to measure the particle pair correlations which are defined as the number of particles of a certain type which are in contact with another particle of another type, normalized by the total number of possible

contacts. The degree dependent pair correlation among unlike particles is given by (see Appendix A.1.1)
$$Q_k^{(ab)} = \rho_k^{(a)} \langle \rho_k^{(b)} \rangle. \tag{3.6}$$
Analogously, the pair correlations among particles of the same type are given by $Q_k^{(aa)} = \rho_k^{(a)} \langle \rho_k^{(a)} \rangle$, showing that the additional term in Eq. (3.4) is caused by the disallowed diffusion steps among particles of the same type. The relevance of this 'jamming' term for the time-evolution can be evaluated by comparing $Q_k^{(aa)}$, which is quadratic in the density, to the corresponding term of the same order, $3\rho^{(a)}\rho_k^{(a)}k/\overline{k}$, by evaluating the ratio
$$\frac{\langle \rho_k^{(a)} \rangle}{3\rho^{(a)}k/\overline{k}} = \frac{\overline{k}}{3k} \frac{\langle \rho_k^{(a)} \rangle}{\rho_k^{(a)}}. \tag{3.7}$$

The one-component analysis reveals that effectively only vertices with a degree $k > k_c$ carry a significant fraction of the particles while vertices with a lower degree have a substantially lower density. In expectation of a similar behavior in the two-component case, the evaluation of the averages in Eq. (3.7) leads to

$$\frac{\langle \rho_k^{(a)} \rangle}{3\rho^{(a)}k/\overline{k}} \approx \frac{1}{3}\frac{\gamma-1}{\gamma-2}\frac{k_c}{k} f(\frac{k_c}{k_{\max}}). \tag{3.8}$$

In this step, the continuous k approximation has been applied to transform the sums of the averages into integrals which were evaluated in the limit of a finite network size which has a maximal degree $k_{\max}$. The scaling function

$$f(x) = \frac{1-x^{\gamma-2}}{1-x^{\gamma-1}} \tag{3.9}$$

has the limiting values

$$f(x) = \begin{cases} 1 & x \to 0 \\ \dfrac{\gamma-2}{\gamma-1} & x \to 1, \end{cases} \tag{3.10}$$

decreasing the importance of the 'jamming' term evenly for all degrees k as it is a monotonically decreasing function for $\gamma > 2$. Due to the k_c/k term in Eq. (3.8), it is suitable to neglect $Q_k^{(aa)}$ for a vertex with $k \gg k_c$. For $k \ll k_c$ both terms, $Q_k^{(aa)}$ and $3k\rho_k^{(a)}\rho^{(a)}/\overline{k}$, are negligible, as these terms are quadratic in the density, being very small for nodes with $k \ll k_c$ in the long-time, low-density limit. The intermediate range of $k \approx k_c$ is difficult to assess analytically, but numerical simulations show that Eq. (3.8) is substantially smaller than 1 in the low density limit even for the range where $k \approx k_c$. Therefore, 'jamming' is only of relevance for vertices with a low degree and high densities. It can be neglected in the following for the calculation of the long-time behavior. In accordance with the approach to the analysis of the

3.1 Reaction-Diffusion Process

one-component dynamics, an expression for the degree resolved particle density $\rho_k^{(a)}$ is obtained by applying a quasi-static approximation to Eq. (3.4), setting $d\rho_k^{(a)}/dt$ equal to 0. This assumes that the diffusion process is much faster and much more frequent than the annihilation reaction which holds in the long-time, low-density limit. This means that the degree resolved densities remain almost constant such that the derivatives vanish. Applying this approximation leads to

$$\rho_k^{(a)} = \frac{\rho^{(a)} k/\overline{k}}{1 + 3\rho^{(a)} k/\overline{k}}. \tag{3.11}$$

This expression for $\rho_k^{(a)}$ has the same structure as found for the $A + A \to \emptyset$ process except that the coefficient of $\rho^{(a)}$ in the denominator is 3 instead of 2. As the structure of the differential equations is the same as for the $A + A \to \emptyset$ process, one obtains the same scaling-behavior of Eq. (3.2) for each component. The new critical k_c for which a vertex is sensed as a hub by the dynamics is

$$k_c = \frac{\overline{k}}{3\rho^{(a)}} = \frac{2\overline{k}}{3\rho}. \tag{3.12}$$

Therefore, for the hubs in the system with $k > k_c$, Eq. (3.11) is close to $1/3$, which is completely consistent with MF analysis, as this means that hubs are occupied by approximately $1/3$ of the time by each component A and B, and are empty for the remaining $1/3$ of the time.

The critical degree k_c defines which vertices serve as hubs for the dynamics, the striking characteristic of the scale-free topology. This critical degree increases constantly with decreasing density, since $k_c \propto 1/\rho^{(a)}$. Consequently, it changes with time which vertices are regarded as hubs by the dynamics. A detailed finite-size discussion by Catanzaro et al. [2005a] reveals that once the critical degree k_c is larger than the maximal degree $k_{\max}$ in the network, the density decay slows down to a linear density decay. As a result, the typical scale-free behavior of a super-linear density decay is only visible for a rather short period of time, making very large system sizes necessary. Furthermore, one might expect that the scaling exponent derived in MF theory for each component's density decay, $f(\gamma) = 1/(\gamma - 2)$, is missing some effects which slow down the reaction for exponents γ close to 2. Otherwise, the diverging $f(\gamma)$ for $\gamma \to 2$ would result in a diverging reaction speed. Clearly, one expects to recover the scaling law given by $f(\gamma)$ for $\gamma \to 3$. Choosing a value of γ which is smaller than but close to 3 has the convenient side effect that the density decay is relatively slow, such that the dynamics will show a 'scale-free' behavior for a longer period of time with the appropriate density decay exponent larger than 1. These considerations for the $A + B \to \emptyset$ process have been verified by numerical simulations for various exponents γ while keeping the system size constant at $N = 10^6$

3 Dynamics on Complex Networks

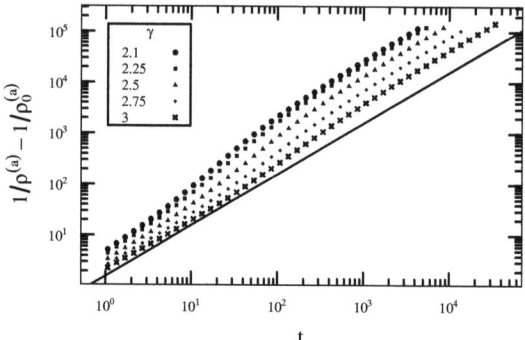

Figure 3.1: Plot showing the density decay of the numerically simulated $A + B \to \emptyset$ process for an initial density $\rho_0 = 0.1$ and different exponents γ. With increasing exponent γ, the density decay behaves 'scale-free' typical for a longer period of time. The solid line has a slope of 1 and is shown as a guide to the eye. Plot is taken from Weber & Porto [2006]

[Weber & Porto, 2006]. The numerical algorithm is described in Appendix A.2.3. Figure 3.1 shows the resulting density decays. The curves deviate from a linear in time decay only for very short durations, but the time span for which each process behaves 'scale-free' increases with increasing exponent γ. An accurate verification of the scaling relation $f(\gamma)$ was therefore performed at a scaling exponent $\gamma = 2.75$, which corresponds to a value of $f = 4/3$, at different system sizes N. Figure 3.2 shows these results, revealing that even for a system size of $N = 10^7$, the density decay shows a scale-free behavior for less then two decades only.

3.1.2 Comparing Network Topologies

To suitably compare the $A + B \to \emptyset$ reaction on different network topologies, some general considerations are inevitable. The previous section highlighted the importance of the scaling exponent γ and the maximal degree $k_{\max}$ in the context of finite scale-free networks. For a meaningful investigation of the impact concerning other topological properties on the dynamics besides these two, it is required to leave these constant and tune the topological property of interest in a controlled manner.

3.1 Reaction-Diffusion Process

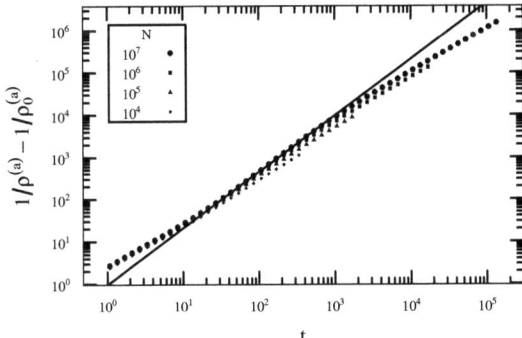

Figure 3.2: Density decay of the numerically simulated $A+B \to \emptyset$ process for uncorrelated networks of various sizes N, exemplified by an exponent $\gamma = 2.75$ and an initial density $\rho_0 = 0.1$. The plot is taken from Weber & Porto [2006] and illustrates the strong finite-size effects of the dynamics.

While this answers the question of what to compare, it still leaves one with the questions of (i) how to quantify the impact and (ii) at what dynamical states to compare the observables. Question (i) is solved by normalizing the measured observable by the value of the corresponding fully randomized case. Concerning the latter question (ii), one commonly compares dynamics at equal times t. This is not favorable for the annihilation dynamics as one particular graph realization (beyond the topological properties discussed here) or initial distribution of particles may speed up or slow down the reaction, altering the dynamical state. Instead, a much better choice is the inverse overall particle density ρ^{-1} which is monotonically increasing. This is supported by the analytical mean-field calculations presented in the previous Sec. 3.1.1. The differential equation (3.5) for the density decay depends solely on the degree resolved particle densities $\rho_k^{(a)}$ and $\rho_k^{(b)}$. These can be approximated in the late-time, low-density limit by Eq. (3.11) with an expression solely determined by the particle density $\rho = 2\rho^{(a)}$ without an explicit time dependence. Additionally, the particle pair correlations $Q_k^{(ab)}$ are exclusively functions of the degree resolved particle densities $\rho_k^{(a)}$ and $\rho_k^{(b)}$. Thus these are also fixed in the late-time limit by the overall particle density.

Using the inverse overall particle density ρ^{-1} instead of time t has the further

3 Dynamics on Complex Networks

advantage that it is possible to define a critical ρ_c^{-1} which marks the crossover from scale-free to non-scale-free behavior of the dynamics on scale-free networks. Once k_c reaches the maximal degree $k_{\max}$ in the network, this crossover occurs which in turn defines

$$\rho_c^{-1} = \frac{3k_{\max}}{2\bar{k}}. \qquad (3.13)$$

The crossover will not be exactly at this value, but it provides a much better approximate than monitoring the scaling exponent f to be greater than 1.

3.1.3 Two-Point Correlations

The framework developed in Sec. 2.2.2 provides the necessary requirements of tunable two-point correlations with a fixed scale-free degree distribution in order to measure the sole influence of two-point correlations. The choice of the average nearest neighbor function $k_{nn}(k) \propto \exp\left[\ln^\alpha\left(1 + \frac{k}{k_{\min}}\right)\right]$ in Sec. 2.2.2, Eq. (2.31) allows to tune the correlation parameter α within a reasonable range. At the same time, this choice is compatible with the required constant maximal degree $k_{\max}$ within the whole range of α used below and does not cause intrinsic degree-degree correlations to arise. The parameter α is chosen such that the resulting networks have a Newman factor r of 0, $\pm r_{\text{low}}$, or $\pm r_{\text{high}}$ ($0 < r_{\text{low}} < r_{\text{high}}$).

The major characteristic of the $A + B \to \emptyset$ reaction besides the density decay is the pattern formation in the form of segregation of the two components. This pattern formation is monitored with the observable

$$Q_{AB} = \frac{N_{AB}}{N_{AA} + N_{BB}}, \qquad (3.14)$$

introduced by Gallos & Argyrakis [2004]. It relates the number of unlike contacts N_{AB} to the total number of like contacts $N_{AA} + N_{BB}$ in each instant, where one contact is counted if two particles are located at adjacent vertices. A decreasing Q_{AB} indicates an ongoing segregation of the reactants.

The Fig. 3.3(a) exemplifies the pattern measure $Q_{AB}(\rho^{-1})$ vs. inverse density ρ^{-1} for an underlying scale-free network with scaling parameter $\gamma = 2.6$ and the initial densities ρ_0 are 0.1 (red symbols) and 0.3 (blue symbols), respectively. As the curves for both initial densities join after a short duration, one can conclude that after this point the process is in each instant in a dynamical state determined solely by the particle density ρ, as predicted by mean-field theory. On the contrary, the pattern measure $Q_{AB}(t)$ vs. time t, as presented in the inset of Fig. 3.3(a), does not reveal this behavior. In Fig. 3.3(b) the pattern formation observable $Q_{AB}(\rho^{-1})$ is shown in relation to the uncorrelated case $Q_{AB}^{uc}(\rho^{-1})$ vs. the inverse density ρ^{-1}. It

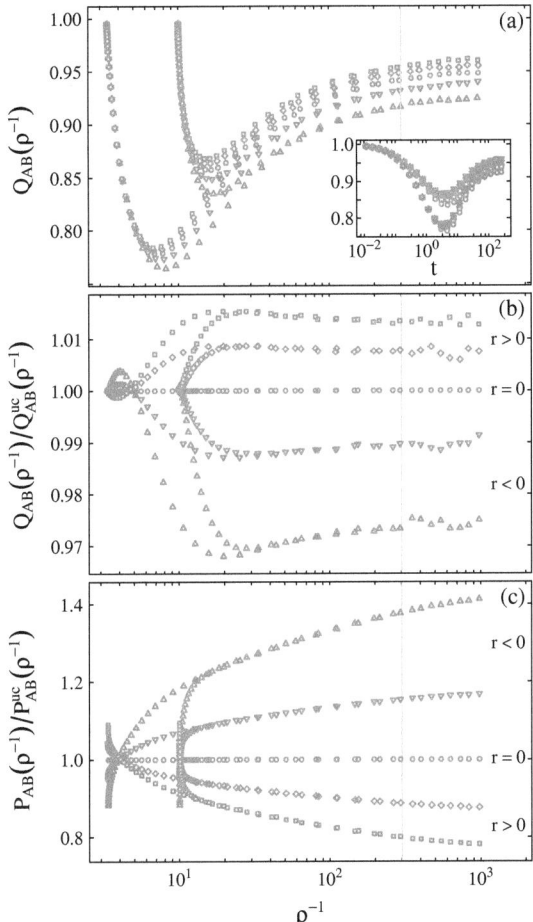

Figure 3.3: (a) Pattern measure $Q_{AB}(\rho^{-1})$ and as inset vs. time t for two-point correlated networks with a scaling parameter $\gamma = 2.6$. (b) Pattern measure $Q_{AB}(\rho^{-1})$ and (c) efficiency measure $P_{AB}(\rho^{-1})$, each normalized to the uncorrelated case. The initial density is 0.3 (red symbols) or 0.1 (blue symbols), the network size is 10^7, and the two-point correlations are by the Newman factor r: $r = r_{\text{high}} = 0.1$ (square), $r = r_{\text{low}} = 0.05$ (diamond), $r = 0$ (circle), $r = -r_{\text{low}}$ (triangle down), $r = -r_{\text{high}}$ (triangle up). Scale-free behavior diminishes past the marked inverse density ρ_c^{-1}. This plot is taken from Weber *et al.* [2008].

3 Dynamics on Complex Networks

is important here to note that the curves settle towards a constant value which is directly related to the strength of two-point correlations, as we show in detail below. The density below which this dynamical equilibration sets in depends on the strength of the correlations and the number of hubs in the network. Dynamics on networks with stronger correlations attain the dynamical equilibrium at lower densities, i.e. larger ρ^{-1}, visible in Fig. 3.3(b) for the $r = \pm r_{\text{high}}$ curves. Equivalent plots of $Q_{\text{AB}}(\rho^{-1})/Q_{\text{AB}}^{\text{uc}}(\rho^{-1})$ for dynamics on networks with smaller scaling parameter values γ than in Fig. 3.3(b) reveal an equilibration at lower densities. The decrease in the scaling parameter γ goes along with an increase in the number of hubs in the system. Consequently, the more hubs present in the system, the lower the density below which an equilibration of $Q_{\text{AB}}(\rho^{-1})/Q_{\text{AB}}^{\text{uc}}(\rho^{-1})$ occurs. However, raising the scaling parameter γ to values greater than 3 prevents pattern equilibration to occur, leading to a non-constant ratio of $Q_{\text{AB}}(\rho^{-1})/Q_{\text{AB}}^{\text{uc}}(\rho^{-1})$ in this case. Apparently, the feature of pattern equilibration is tied to a diverging second moment of the degree distribution.

From Fig. 3.3(b) a pronounced segregation in the disassortative case can be inferred, since the curves for $r < 0$ fall below unity when compared to the uncorrelated case $r = 0$. Counterintuitively, simulations show a much faster reaction on these disassortative networks. This apparent contradiction between segregation and high reaction speed is resolved by observing a new quantity

$$P_{\text{AB}} = \frac{\# \text{ annihilations}}{\# \text{ created } AB \text{ contacts}}, \qquad (3.15)$$

which measures at each instant how efficient the reaction performs as it directly quantifies how many annihilations take place per created unlike contacts. Figure 3.3(c) illustrates $P_{\text{AB}}(\rho^{-1})$ in relation to the uncorrelated case. The reactions running on disassortative networks show a strongly increased efficiency as these curves lie well above unity. The increase in efficiency for disassortatively correlated networks is even one order of magnitude larger than the decrease in the measure $Q_{\text{AB}}(\rho^{-1})$ (indicating segregation), and is thus the dominating effect, explaining the accelerated reaction speed.

The very interesting observation of a constant ratio $Q_{\text{AB}}/Q_{\text{AB}}^{\text{uc}}$ for small densities allows one to measure directly the dynamical response under a topological change of the network by means of pattern formation with a single number. The constant ratio is therefore a good measure to quantify the dynamical impact of the two-point degree-degree correlations. In Fig. 3.4(a) this dynamical response is shown for different choices of the scaling parameter γ. The data is plotted against the *a priori* fixed correlation parameter α and shown as a function of the resulting Newman factor r in the inset. One observes a linear relation of the pattern formation constant $Q_{\text{AB}}/Q_{\text{AB}}^{\text{uc}}$

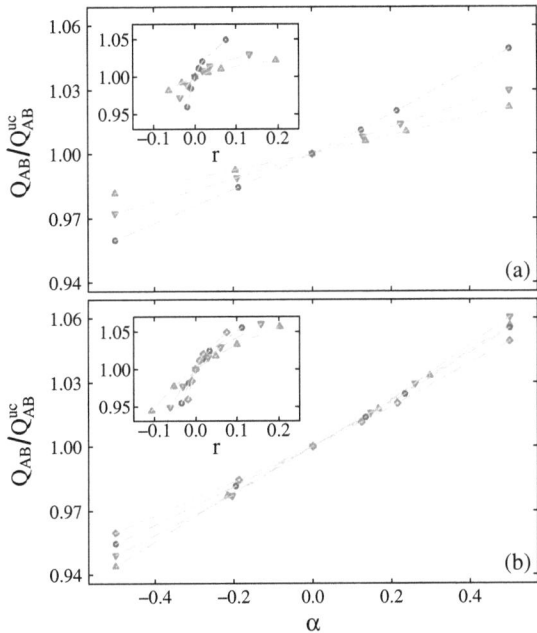

Figure 3.4: Dynamical response of the $A + B \to \emptyset$ reaction with respect to the pattern formation measure Q_{AB}/Q_{AB}^{uc} as a function of the parameter α, which is used in the average nearest neighbor function $k_{nn}(k)$. (a) Results for a system size of $N = 10^7$ with different values of the scaling parameter γ for the underlying scale-free network: $\gamma = 2.4$ (triangle up), $\gamma = 2.6$ (triangle down), and $\gamma = 2.8$ (circle). (b) System size dependency of the pattern formation measure Q_{AB}/Q_{AB}^{uc} exemplified for the scaling parameter $\gamma = 2.8$: $N = 10^4$ (triangle up), $N = 10^5$ (triangle down), $N = 10^6$ (circle), and $N = 10^7$ (diamond). The respective inset in each figure presents the data vs. the Newman factor r. The plot is taken from Weber et al. [2008].

and the correlation parameter α. The slope of this linear inter-relationship increases with increasing scale parameter γ. This linearity is only observed if the data is plotted against the correlation parameter α which turns out to be a better choice than the Newman factor r to measure the strength of the two-point degree-degree correlations regarding the dynamical response. Even though the parameter α is not a general statistical measure, it is capable of describing the overall correlations quite well. This becomes clear in Fig. 3.4(b), where we exemplify the finite-size effects on the pattern formation Q_{AB}/Q_{AB}^{uc} vs. the correlation parameter α for the scaling parameter $\gamma = 2.8$. The network size N has been varied over 3 magnitudes, and one expects a data-collapse such that all points fall onto a single line, independent of the network size N as the quantity Q_{AB}/Q_{AB}^{uc} is by definition free of finite-size effects. Fig. 3.4(b) verifies this expectation for small values of the correlation parameter α and only minor deviations are noticeable from the data-collapse for very strong correlations. The inset plot in Fig. 3.4(b) shows the same function versus the resulting Newman factor r, where the functional dependence changes with the network size N.

3.2 Prisoner's Dilemma

The Prisoner's Dilemma game is motivated by the question of sustaining cooperation within populations of unrelated individuals where selfish actions are rewarded and there is no kin selection. The game in the form studied here originates from the field of evolutionary game theory Weibull [1995]. This framework emerged out of the combination of the two concepts evolution and game theory. The evolution is concerned about the development of populations consisting out of individuals which have a fitness ascribed. The fitness of an individual quantifies the reproduction rate of that individual, thus causing a selection. A higher fitness than the average fitness therefore leads to a higher density of such individuals within a population. The fitness of each individual is determined by the payoff which the individuals receive by playing a game against others. Within such games multiple individuals can interact. Reducing the number of interacting players to two is a common scenario studied in game theory, but still captures the essential aspects.

Game Theory The key concept of game theory is the use of a strategy set $\mathcal{S}$ from which players must choose from within a game. The player's payoff depends on the choice of its own and the choice of the opponents strategy. A game is defined by a set of participating players, a set of strategies $\mathcal{S}$ and a payoff function which defines the payoffs resulting from different matchings of respective strategies chosen

3.2 Prisoner's Dilemma

by players. Supposing a two-player game with two strategies, $\mathcal{S} = \{C, D\}$, to choose from, these matchings can be described by the scheme,

	C	D
C	R	S
D	T	P

If the first player selects C and the second also selects C, then both receive a payoff R, respectively for mutual selection of D both receive P. In case the first player selects C while the other selects D, then the first will get S and the second player will receive T. This particular scheme assigns the payoffs to each player by the same rules. The game belongs to the important class of a symmetric two-player game. The payoffs of a two-player game are representable by a payoff matrix M, which has the form in the case of the 2 strategy game above

$$M = \begin{pmatrix} R & S \\ T & P \end{pmatrix}. \tag{3.16}$$

In general, the payoff matrix M is for a symmetric two-player game with n strategies defined by a $n \times n$ matrix with the entries m_{ij}.

Given the opponents strategy, a strategy is said to be a best reply if no other strategy earns a higher payoff. A cornerstone of game theory is the concept of a Nash equilibrium [Nash, 1950a,b, 1951] which is the set of strategies which are best replies to themselves. Equivalently, if a strategy is played, which belongs to a Nash equilibrium, then no other strategy will yield a higher payoff. The Prisoner's Dilemma game is characterized by the ordering of the scores within the payoff matrix M. If C represents the strategy cooperation and D the defection strategy, the ordering of the scores in the Prisoner's Dilemma is $T > R > P > S$. In such a setup the defect strategy D is advantageous for an individual player as it will in each round yield the chance for a higher payoff. The cooperator strategy C is said to be dominated by the defector strategy D, since choosing strategy D guarantees to yield a higher or equal payoff than the other player. Since changing to another strategy than defect D results in a lowered payoff, it is also a Nash equilibrium.

A major concern of game theory is to classify strategies and strategy profiles. The Nash equilibrium is probably the most important one. However, placing game theory within the concept of evolution shifts the focus into a different direction. Incorporating the concept of evolution requires the introduction of populations of players which play certain strategies. Thus, a distinct fraction of players play distinct strategies. The common scenario within evolutionary game theory is the assumption of a large population within which randomly drawn players are matched pairwise to play a game. An important case in biology is the special situation of a large homogeneous population. The homogeneity is understood in the sense that all individuals play the same strategy $i \in \mathcal{S}$. Supposing now, a small fraction $\varepsilon \in (0,1)$ of mutant individuals which play strategy $j \in \mathcal{S}, j \neq i$ enter such a homogeneous population. Evolution is assumed to select the strategy which will yield a higher fitness. The question whether strategy i will resist a mutant strategy j depends on the conditions: (i) The payoff from strategy i when played against itself must return a payoff which is higher or equal to the payoff when strategy i is played against any other strategy, say j. (ii) If the payoff of i played against itself is equal to the payoff returned if i plays against another strategy j, then the payoff from j played against itself must be lower than the payoff of i playing against itself. Whenever a strategy fulfills these conditions, it is said to be an evolutionary stable strategy (ESS) [Maynard Smith, 1974, 1982, Maynard Smith & Price, 1973], an integral concept of evolutionary game theory. To formalize these ideas, let ρ_i denote the fraction of players which hold on to strategy i. Given the densities $\rho_j, j \in \mathcal{S}$ of all present strategies in a population, the expected average payoff for each strategy $i \in \mathcal{S}$ is then

$$u_i = \sum_{j \in \mathcal{S}} \rho_j \, m_{ij}, \qquad (3.17)$$

where the coefficients m_{ij} are the entries of the payoff matrix M. With such a definition the ESS criteria translates for a strategy i into the inequality

$$\varepsilon_j \, m_{ij} + (1 - \varepsilon_j) \, m_{ii} > \varepsilon_j \, m_{jj} + (1 - \varepsilon_j) \, m_{ji}. \qquad (3.18)$$

The density of the mutant strategy j is denoted by ε_j such that the density of the homogeneous strategy i is $1 - \varepsilon_j$.

Evolutionary Game Theory A mathematical implementation of the idea that evolution proposes the reproduction of individuals proportional to their fitness has been introduced by Taylor [1979] with the replicator dynamics. Assuming a population within which individuals are pairwise randomly matched and reproduction takes places continuously over time, the resulting differential equation for the changing fractions ρ_i of players which play a strategy i is

$$\frac{d\rho_i}{dt} = \rho_i(u_i - \phi). \qquad (3.19)$$

Here, ϕ is the average payoff of the whole population

$$\phi = \sum_{i \in \mathcal{S}} \rho_i u_i. \qquad (3.20)$$

3.2 Prisoner's Dilemma

Consequently, the fraction of individuals which play a strategy that yields a payoff larger than the average of the whole population will increase over time.

The replicator dynamics assumes a well-mixed population within which every player may play with any other. In the case of the Prisoner's Dilemma such an all-to-all interaction pattern always results in a population consisting only out of defectors. Restricting the interactions from all-to-all, which corresponds to a mean-field scenario, to regular structures such as lattices where players are at the lattice sites and interactions are only possible among adjacent sites, reveals that cooperation can sustain, although only rather small fractions of the population hold on to the cooperation strategy in the stationary state which will emerge.

Generalizing the underlying topology to a network where vertices are players and restricting interactions to adjacent players defined by the edges results in the astonishing phenomenon that cooperation may even dominate the defect strategy on networks with a scale-free degree distribution. The strong impact the degree distribution $P(k)$ has on the level of sustained cooperation has recently been studied numerically by Gomez-Gardenes et al. [2007a] on Barabási-Albert and Erdős-Rényi networks. The authors investigated the Prisoner's Dilemma with the parameters $R = 1$, $P = S = 0$, $T = b > 1$. The choice of these parameters follows common practice [Nowak et al., 2004, Santos & Pacheco, 2005] to rescale the Prisoner's Dilemma to an effective one-parameter version. The parameter b sets the temptation to defect. The evolution has been implemented with a finite population analogue of the replicator dynamics [Santos & Pacheco, 2005].

Cumulative Payoffs In each time step, every individual i plays with its adjacent neighbors and accumulates the payoff

$$\pi_i = \sum_j a_{ij}\, \pi(i,j). \tag{3.21}$$

Here, $\pi(i,j)$ denotes the payoff from a single game the player i receives when playing with j. The sum in Eq. (3.21) will accumulate the results from k_i games, since the player i has degree k_i. Following this, all players update their strategy synchronously by comparing their individual payoff π_i with the payoff π_j of a randomly chosen adjacent player j. The strategy s_j of the player j is adopted by player i with the probability

$$P(s_i \to s_j) = \begin{cases} \dfrac{\pi_j - \pi_i}{b\,\max(k_i, k_j)} & \text{if } \pi_j - \pi_i > 0 \\ 0 & \text{otherwise} \end{cases}. \tag{3.22}$$

Initially all players are set with a probability of $p = 1/2$ to play either the cooperation or the defection strategy. For the initial transient, the system is evolved for a fixed

3 Dynamics on Complex Networks

time frame and consecutively an appropriate test whether the the stationary state has been reach is applied. A rigorous test how to detect whether the system is in the stationary state is not agreed on in the literature. The method used here is explained in the Appendix A.2.4. Consecutively, the system is evolved for further 10^4 time steps during which observables are recorded. In particular the density of cooperators ρ is measured.

Of special interest are players which do not change their strategy during the observation period. These players have associated pure densities as pure cooperator density ρ_c and pure defector density ρ_d. These stable pure cooperating players are very important in the sustainment of cooperation. Conseqeuently, the number of components C_c within a network which are made up of solely pure cooperators is also very important and is monitored as well. Gomez-Gardenes et al. [2007a] performed the numerical simulations on Erdős-Rényi graphs of size $N = 4000$ with an average degree $\overline{k} = 4$ and Barabási-Albert networks of the same size and the same average degree $\overline{k}$. The striking result is the dominance of the cooperation strategy for a wide range of the parameter b in the case of the scale-free Barabási-Albert network. The Erdős-Rényi networks in comparison perform much worse. A detailed examination reveals that the cooperator density ρ is to a large fraction made up of pure cooperators which form a single connected component in the case of Barabási-Albert networks. Thus, the number of pure cooperator components C_c is exactly 1 over the whole parameter range of b checked in Gomez-Gardenes et al. [2007a] for the Barabási-Albert networks. The Erdős-Rényi networks, on the contrary, have many of these components. The authors argue that the scale-free structure of the Barabási-Albert network is to be claimed for the well support of cooperation in this topology as hubs are held to be responsible for the high cooperation density. However, a thorough review of these results regarding the Barabási-Albert networks, see Pusch et al. [2008b], reveals that the particular structure of the Barabási-Albert networks is responsible for many of the observations. Due to the stepwise preferential attachment scheme used to create the Barabási-Albert networks, a large and heavily connected component builds up around the oldest vertices within the network. The oldest vertices in turn do have the major fraction of edges and will in general be the vertices with the largest degree, i.e. these vertices can be regarded as the hubs of the network. This explains the peculiarity of the exclusive existence of only one purely cooperating component. In addition, it is most likely that all hubs within the Barabási-Albert networks are connected to each other which stabilizes cooperation.

Hubs, vertices with a large degree k, are stabilized due to the special updating rules of Eq. (3.22) used within this version of the Prisoner's Dilemma game. The reasons are two-fold as the normalization factor $b\max(k_i, k_j)$ is very large for hubs, making a strategy adoption unlikely. However, the major stabilization factor roots in the accumulation of payoffs in Eq. (3.21). Just by the large degree k a hub attains a much higher payoff in total, since payoffs are simply added up. Therefore, hubs have very likely a larger payoff than their adjacent vertices with a lower degree k and become inert against a strategy adoption. Even if two hubs with a comparable degree and opposing strategies are connected to each other, a persuasion of one another is unlikely since hubs have many neighbors to which they possibly compare themselves.

Effective Payoffs The stabilization of cooperation is evidently due to the accumulation of payoffs. This accumulation is also responsible for breaking the invariance under positive affine transformations of the payoffs inherent to the replicator dynamics as described in Eq. (3.19). A positive affine transformation to the average payoffs u_i is defined by two arbitrary constant parameters $\alpha > 0$ and $\beta \in \mathcal{R}$. The new average payoff u_i' for an individual playing strategy i is

$$u_i' = \alpha u_i + \beta. \tag{3.23}$$

Inserting this altered average payoff into Eq. (3.19) gives a differential equation of

$$\frac{d\rho_i}{d(\alpha t)} = \rho_i(u_i - \phi). \tag{3.24}$$

The positive affine transformation only changes the time scale, but leaves the characteristics of the dynamics unchanged. To observe how such a positive affine transformation alters the discrete replicator dynamics on networks, it is convenient to introduce the definitions

$$D = \max(T, R, P, S) - \min(T, R, P, S) \tag{3.25}$$
$$k_> = \max(k_i, k_j). \tag{3.26}$$

With these the adoption probability of Eq. (3.22) can be rewritten as

$$P(s_i \to s_j) = \begin{cases} \dfrac{\pi_j - \pi_i}{D\, k_>} & \text{if } \pi_j - \pi_i > 0 \\ 0 & \text{otherwise} \end{cases}. \tag{3.27}$$

The payoff π_i of a player i within a network which has k_i edges connected to it will have a transformed payoff

$$\pi_i' = \alpha\, \pi_i + \beta\, k_i. \tag{3.28}$$

This changes the adoption probability into

$$P'(s_i \to s_j) = \begin{cases} P(s_i \to s_j) + \beta \dfrac{k_j - k_i}{\alpha D k_>} & \text{if } \pi_j' - \pi_i' > 0 \\ 0 & \text{otherwise} \end{cases}. \tag{3.29}$$

3 Dynamics on Complex Networks

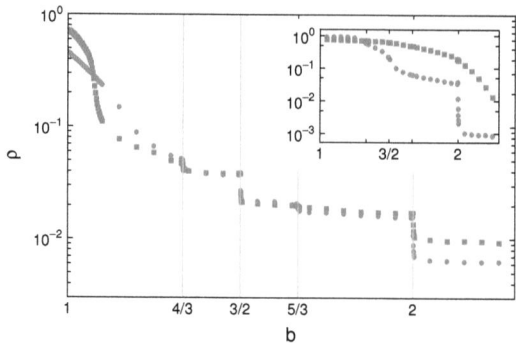

Figure 3.5: Cooperator density ρ for effective payoff rules on a scale-free network with scaling exponent $\gamma = 3$ (square) along with the corresponding Erdős-Rényi network (circle). The inset shows the analogous results for cumulative payoffs.

This property inherent to an accumulation of payoffs in this context has first been pointed out by Tomassini et al. [2007] and an alternative approach was proposed, the concept of an 'average payoff'. The authors suggest to normalize the payoff π_i of each player i by the degree k_i of the player, resulting in a so-called 'average payoff'

$$\tilde{\pi}_i = \frac{1}{k_i} \sum_j a_{ij}\, \pi(i,j). \qquad (3.30)$$

The payoff $\tilde{\pi}_i$ can be regarded as an efficiency score. Using these effective payoffs recovers the invariance of the replicator dynamics with respect to positive affine transformations again. Tomassini et al. [2007] focus on the transient properties of the dynamics and a further study concerning this version of the Prisoner's Dilemma on Barabási-Albert networks is available [Szolnoki et al., 2008]. A publication concerning the efficiency ruled strategy spreading on scale-free networks with two-point correlations is in preparation [Weber & Porto, 2009a]. In the following, the results for both versions will be presented.

Switching to effective payoffs reveals drastic changes in the dynamics as numerical simulations show. These were performed on scale-free networks of size $N = 4000$ and a scale exponent $\gamma = 3$ for comparability with results from Gomez-Gardenes et al. [2007a], see the Appendix A.2.4 for implementation details. In Fig. 3.5 the cooperator density ρ in case of efficiency ruled payoffs for a scale-free network (square)

3.2 Prisoner's Dilemma

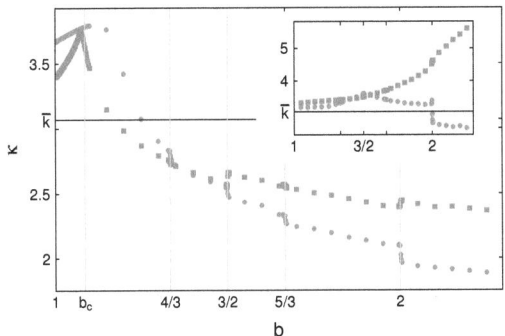

Figure 3.6: Average degree of cooperating players κ for effective payoffs and as an inset for cumulative payoffs. Symbols are as in Fig. 3.5.

and a corresponding Erdős-Rényi network (circle) with the same average degree of $\bar{k} = 3.06$ is shown along with respective data as inset for the cumulative payoffs. As a result of the efficiency ruled payoffs, the advantage of the scale-free topology over an Erdős-Rényi structure disappears for a wide range of the parameter b. However, for very large values of b, the scale-free topology becomes advantageous again over the Erdős-Rényi network and even out-performs the cooperator density ρ for the accumulated payoff version. While the efficiency ruled strategy spreading version of the Prisoner's Dilemma game drops to densities as low as 10^{-2} for values of b larger than 2, the accumulated payoffs version drops one magnitude of order lower. In addition, discontinuities in the cooperator density ρ become visible for rational values of b. These arise from interactions among connected vertices with corresponding degrees. Exactly at the discontinuities, stable interactions among pure cooperators and pure defectors build up which has been verified by monitoring the number of edges among these type of players explicitly. This number of edges is zero for all values of b except at the rational values of b for which the discontinuities are observed in Fig. 3.5.

The use of effective payoffs drastically alters the dynamics and the characteristics of the stationary state. By introduction of the effective payoffs, the vertices with large degree k loose their inertness against strategy adoption. Monitoring the average degree of cooperating players κ, which is presented in Fig. 3.6, reveals that with increasing b cooperation tends to be exhibited by players with lower degrees k. The noticeable sudden decrease of κ close to 1 reveals a critical benefit b_c which

3 Dynamics on Complex Networks

is due to the maximal degree $k_{\max}$ within the finite network. The concept of effective payoffs turns every player into the equivalent situation of playing their chosen strategy against a population of k other players in each time step. The concepts from evolutionary game theory apply commonly, and in particular the ESS concept, within the case of an infinitely large population size $N_p \to \infty$. The definition of ESS claims the stability of a strategy i against an infinitesimal small fraction ε_j of a mutant strategy j into an infinitely large population. Within a finite population a new phenomena of neutral drift emerges. Supposing a population to consist out of $N_p - 1$ individuals playing strategy i and 1 mutant which sticks to strategy j. If both strategies i and j yield the same fitness, then j can replace i with a probability of $1/N_p$. The concept of a finite evolutionary stable strategy ESS_N introduced by Nowak et al. [2004] incorporates this feature of neutral drift inherent to finite populations. An ESS_N strategy must oppose an invasion and the replacement by neutral drift of another strategy [Nowak, 2006, Nowak et al., 2004]. Applying this concept to the effective payoff version of the Prisoner's Dilemma game reveals that the defector strategy will always be in the set of ESS_N while the cooperator strategy is in this set if the population size N_p, which corresponds to the degree k of a vertex, fulfills the condition

$$b < \frac{k+1}{k-2}. \tag{3.31}$$

At the critical benefit b_c this condition becomes invalid even for the vertices with the largest degree $k_{\max}$ within the network which defines the critical benefit

$$b_c = \frac{k_{\max}+1}{k_{\max}-2}. \tag{3.32}$$

Once b is lower than b_c, the cooperator strategy is in the set of ESS_N for all vertices in the network. This will in turn cause a decrease of κ in direction to the much lower average degree $\overline{k}$, since cooperation is now capable to spread over the complete network such that cooperators will on average populate vertices with the average degree $\overline{k}$.

The decrease of κ with large values of b is in striking contrast to the accumulated payoff version. The corresponding curve in the inset of Fig. 3.6 on the preceding page shows a clear shift towards a larger average degree κ of cooperating players in the case of scale-free networks. Therefore, vertices with a small degree k are important in the sustainment of cooperation for effective payoffs. The scale-free networks perform better since there are simply much more vertices with a low degree available than there are in the case of Erdős-Rényi networks with the same average degree. This strongly opposes the frequent result in the context of scale-free networks that the hubs of the network are held to be responsible for some peculiarity.

3.2 Prisoner's Dilemma

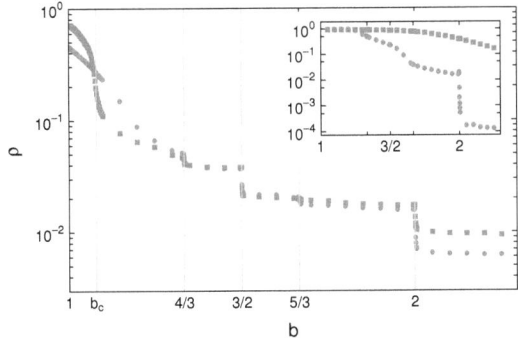

Figure 3.7: Cooperator density ρ in case of effective payoffs shown for a lower value of the scale-exponent $\gamma = 2.5$ along with the respective Erdős-Rényi network. Symbols correspond to Fig. 3.5 and the inset shows the cumulative payoff case.

However, the scale-free structure still seems to be of importance, since lowering the value of γ to a value of 2.5 increases the level of cooperation in both versions as shown in Fig. 3.7. It is crucial to note that the overall average degree $\bar{k}$ increases to a value of 3.85 such that the dynamics should behave more like in the mean-field case, meaning that cooperation is suppressed. The Erdős-Rényi networks follow this expectation, displaying a decreased level of cooperation.

3.2.1 Two-Point Correlations

Strong assortativity and clustering is frequently observed within social networks like friendship networks. An impact of these network properties on the Prisoner's Dilemma is therefore expected. Repeating numerical simulations for both versions of the game with disassortative, uncorrelated, and assortative scale-free networks by tuning correlations as introduced in Sec. 2.2.2 reveals contrary behavior. The cooperator density dependence ρ on the correlation parameter α in the case of effective payoffs is shown in Fig. 3.8 on the next page along with an inset which shows the number of pure cooperating components C_c. For values of $b > b_c$ the assortative networks show a decreased level of cooperation. As argued above, the vertices with a large degree k are not accessible for cooperators, since the cooperator strategy is not in the set of ESS_N for degrees which do not comply with the condition of Eq. (3.31).

3 Dynamics on Complex Networks

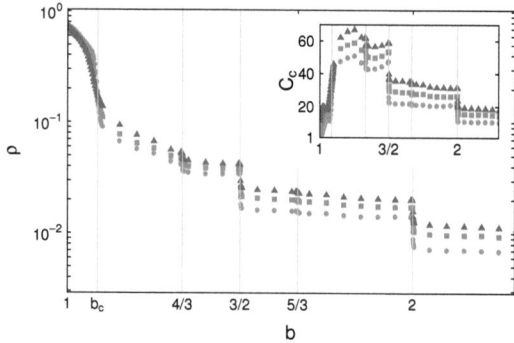

Figure 3.8: Dependence of the cooperator density ρ in the effective payoff case on two-point correlations set by α equals to 0 (square), 0.2 (circle), and -0.2 (triangle). The scale-free network has a scaling exponent of $\gamma = 3$. The inset shows the number of pure cooperating components C_c.

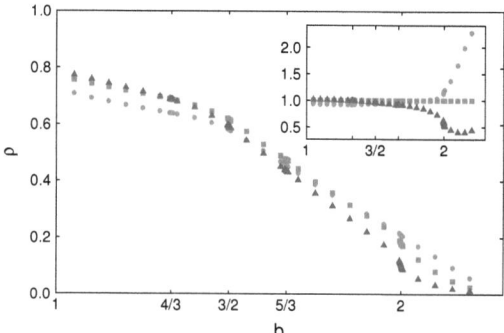

Figure 3.9: Impact of two-point correlations within a scale-free network with $\gamma = 3$ on the cooperator density ρ for cumulative payoffs. Symbols correspond to Fig. 3.8 and the inset shows the data relative against the uncorrelated case of $\alpha = 0$.

Assortative networks result in an increased connectedness of degrees of the same order, especially of those with large degree. This makes an invasion of cooperators onto vertices with a large degree k or the sustainment of the cooperator strategy even more unlikely on these high degree nodes. The direct neighborhood of these high degree vertices is biased towards the defection strategy. Tuning the correlations in the opposite direction, on the other hand, brings up more players with a lower degree k in the direct neighborhood of large degree vertices. The cooperators profit from this as they now have a higher chance of invading a large degree vertex since the support from other cooperating players on low degree vertices in the direct neighborhood is increased. In accordance with this, the number of components with pure cooperators is strongly enhanced by disassortativity, a consequence of the altered cooperator density which spreads into niches of the network. The picture changes once the temptation to defect falls below b_c. In this regime, the cooperator strategy is in the set of ESS_N for all vertices, making all vertices accessible to the cooperation strategy, including the large degree vertices. The large degree vertices are of exceptional importance for the connectivity within the network. With the increasing density of cooperators on these large degree vertices, the number of pure cooperator components C_c collapses as these become aggregated to large components. This aggregation to large components of pure cooperators stabilizes cooperation. The aggregation is occurring faster on assortative networks which ultimately results in an increased cooperator density in the assortative case for values of b below b_c.

Two-point correlations conversely alter the cooperation density ρ in the accumulated payoff version of the Prisoner's Dilemma game as shown in Fig. 3.9. The key property of the accumulated payoff version of the game is the resulting inertness of vertices with a high degree against strategy adoption. This causes the adoption of the respective strategy by the nodes within the direct neighborhood of these high degree nodes. The increased cooperator density ρ up to a factor of 2 for assortative networks in the regime of very high values of b roots in the amplification of the inertness for the cooperator nodes. Supposing a cooperator and a defector to be initially connected. Both are assumed to have a large degree of the same order and to have a distinct neighborhood. Initially both vertices will spread their respective strategy to their direct neighborhood. Once the defector has done so, he will no longer receive a high payoff in contrast to the cooperating player. Effectively the defector has only a short time window available to turn the high degree cooperator into a defector, otherwise the cooperator will have a higher payoff and will turn the defector into a cooperator. This mechanism explains why assortativity enhances cooperation for large values of b and explains the substantial increase in the average degree of cooperators κ.

The situation for values of b close to 1 is different, as in this regime the survival of defectors is promoted in regions with cliques of small degree vertices which are more frequent in assortative networks.

3.2.2 Clustering

The consequences of clustering, which is regulated by two-point correlations, were studied in the context of uncorrelated networks with a value of α set to 0 in the ansatz presented in Sec. 2.2.2. Surprisingly, the version of effective payoffs does not display any dependence on clustering. Dynamical correlations further than two vertices are therefore absent and do not build up. Thus, two-point correlations are solely induced by the interaction rules which is in full accordance with the picture depicted in the above Sec. 3.2 that each vertex in the network is equivalent to a population of k players. The averaging procedure used to obtain the effective payoffs consequently results in mean-field like behavior.

In the context of the accumulated payoffs, enhanced clustering interestingly supports the inferior strategy. In Fig. 3.10 the cooperator density ρ is presented. Up to a cooperator density of 0.5 a decreased cooperator density is caused by clustering, while starting from this density the enhanced clustering increases the cooperator density. The inset of Fig. 3.10 shows the cooperator density ρ in relation to the unclustered network. The plot reveals that clustering strongly increases the cooperator density within the vicinity of large values for b. This effect roots in an intensified inertness against strategy adoption. Once the situation arises that three cooperating vertices are connected to each other to form a triangle, they support and stabilize each other. Conceptually, a triangle of cooperators can be replaced by a single vertex which combines all edges which leave these three vertices. This in turn increases the effective degree of these vertices, growing their inertness and stability. Due to this mechanism, the number of pure cooperating components C_c increases by clustering which is shown in Fig. 3.11. While for uncorrelated networks without clustering only 1 pure cooperating component exists, cooperation is spread to other niches within the network in case clustering is enhanced. The strong discontinuities at $b = 2$ are caused by the stable interactions among pure cooperators and defectors at this integer value of b, as discussed above.

3.3 Conclusion

The challenge of a meaningful comparison of dynamics on different network topologies has been successfully solved for the two dynamics in question. In a first step

3.3 Conclusion

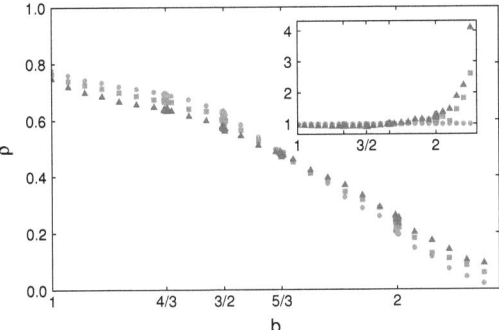

Figure 3.10: Influence of clustering for accumulated cooperation dynamics on the density of cooperators ρ. The scale-free network has a scaling exponent $\gamma = 3$ and the clustering is tuned to μ equals 0 (circle), 0.1 (square), and 0.2 (triangle). The inset shows the curves in relation to the unclustered data.

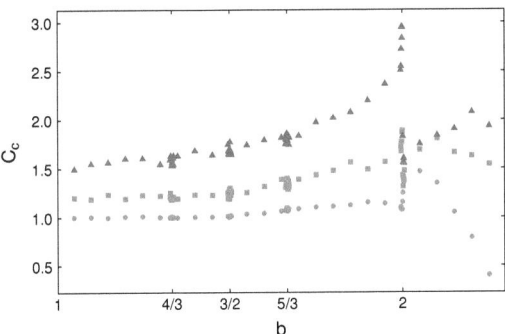

Figure 3.11: Number of pure cooperating components C_c for the accumulated payoff version on a scale-free network with different levels of clustering as in Fig. 3.10 with according symbols.

3 Dynamics on Complex Networks

major topological constraints were identified. Within the context of scale-free networks the dependence on the scaling exponent γ and the importance of the maximal degree $k_{\max}$ were identified. While the scaling exponent γ ultimately determines the dynamics behavior in both dynamics studied, the maximal degree $k_{\max}$ is responsible for finite-size effects. These topological properties are required to be held fixed in order to study the impact of two-point correlations and clustering.

A further question, arising particularly in the $A + B \to \emptyset$ reaction-diffusion process, is related to the dynamical states by which the dynamics can be compared on different topologies. The common parameter time turns out to be unsuitable and has to be abandoned in favor of the inverse particle density ρ^{-1}. This is supported by the analytical calculations for the uncorrelated case in Sec. 3.1.1, showing that the density fixes all relevant system properties in the long-time, low-density limit. Monitoring the pattern formation in the two-component diffusion-annihilation reveals that the effect of two-point correlations can be captured by a single scalar value. Exploiting this fact identifies the correlation parameter α as a better measure than the Newman factor r to describe the dynamical impact of two-point correlations on the dynamics. The Newman factor suffers from finite-size effects while the correlation parameter α is free from such a short-coming.

The observed super-linear density decay in the diffusion-annihilation process on scale-free networks with a scaling exponent γ in the range of $(2, 3]$ is caused by the existence of hubs, nodes with a large degree k. Which degree k is sufficiently large to consider a vertex as a hub is determined by the decreasing particle density.

In accordance with these results, the dominant role of hubs is strongly emphasized in the accumulated payoff version of the Prisoner's Dilemma game. A large degree k causes inertness against strategy adoption which is responsible for the stabilization of the cooperator density. This advantage vanishes in the effective payoff version of the game. As a result the vertices with a small degree become the prevalent ones. The contrary influence of two-point correlations on the accumulated and the effective payoff version underlines the fundamental differences these two dynamics exhibit. However, while two-point correlations support either strategy over the whole range of the temptation to defect parameter b, enhanced clustering selectively supports the inferior strategy in the accumulated payoff game.

4 Evolution of Networks

The concept of evolution [Nowak, 2006] from the domain of biology is ideally suited to study the impact a dynamical process has on a network topology. Within this framework a population of individuals reproduces itself in consecutive generations. A reproduction of an individual involves the duplication of the parent, passing all properties of the parent to the offspring. Rarely the duplication occurs with some errors or modifications, yielding a mutant individual with distinct properties. Then, selection regulates at what rates the distinct individuals reproduce themselves and ultimately controls which type of individuals survives. In the context of a network evolution, a distinct individual is represented by a distinct network realization and the selection mechanism controls the reproduction of these on the basis of fitness scores which are determined by the dynamical processes on these network realizations. This scheme implements a feedback from the dynamics on the network topology and allows to identify the optimal network topologies for the given fitness criteria. The evolution considered here is performed with the aim to find these optimal network topologies. An integral assumption within this ansatz is the separated time-scale of the evolution from the dynamics since the network realization is held fixed during every dynamics.

In order to carry out the desired network evolution, a network mutation and a network selection mechanism are required. The network mutation procedure has to induce small random variations within the original network and fulfill some constraints, i.e. being ergodic within the network configuration space. Two appropriate schemes are presented and evaluated in Sec. 4.1. This is followed by the introduction of the selection process which originates from the domain of biology and is mapped onto the concepts of statistical physics [Sella & Hirsh, 2005]. The results for the two dynamical processes considered are presented in Sec. 4.2. The chapter closes with a conclusion.

4.1 Network Mutation

The concepts of mutation and selection are independent in the course of an evolution. This requires the network mutation to act on a network without the knowledge

4 Evolution of Networks

of the dynamics. Including the knowledge of the dynamics within a network mutation step would bias the evolution *a priori* into some direction. Instead, the network mutation must allow for an ergodic random diffusion within the network configuration space. The network configuration space is of enormous size and it is therefore desirable to use a mutation scheme which is capable to produce random mutant networks following the direction within the network configuration space induced by the selection mechanism. By the independence from the selection mechanism, the mutation scheme can not use any information provided by the dynamics. Assuming that a particular dynamics is supported by distinct correlation patterns, the mutation mechanism should support the build up of distinct conformations, i.e. the increase of two-point correlations, clustering, and others, given a distinct network realization. The mechanism should support any type of patterns and must not be bound to a particular class of networks.

The first ansatz investigated removed a small fraction of randomly chosen edges from the network and added these again in a random manner. While it seems very intuitive, this attempt fails immediately as this scheme drives every network realization into an Erdős-Rényi type graph. This highlights a further aspect to consider, the random mutation scheme must not be bound to some particular class of networks, but allow for an ergodic sampling of the network configuration space. Complete redistribution of all edges at random within each mutation would certainly ensure an ergodic mutation, but the probability to yield networks with a degree distribution different than a Poissonian is extremely unlikely. Necessarily, the mutation scheme has to take into account the complete network realization and induce, based on this information, some small perturbations.

Two schemes implementing these considerations are introduced below. To assure that these mutation mechanisms meet the requirements presented above, each scheme is thoroughly evaluated. To ensure the ergodic property, distinct network realizations are successively mutated, but only mutations are accepted which minimize the topological distance between the current network realization and an a priori fixed network topology. The topological distance

$$d = \sum_{j,k} \left| P(j' \geq j, k' \geq k) - P^{\text{t}}(j' \geq j, k' \geq k) \right| \qquad (4.1)$$

is defined in terms of the joint degree distribution from the network realization, $P(j,k)$, and the joint degree distribution $P^{\text{t}}(j,k)$ of the a priori fixed target network. The use of cumulative statistics is necessary for reasons explained in Sec. 2.3 since the distance is determined among realizations of single network realizations. Choosing the initial and the target network to be vastly different allows to explicitly test the ability of a mutation scheme to turn an Erdős-Rényi network into a scale-free

4.1 Network Mutation

network with pre-scribed two-point correlations or vice versa. While this testing scheme is by no means sufficient to ensure full ergodicity, it is sufficient to test whether the scheme is capable to attain large variations in the degree sequence and has the capacity to build up two-point correlations which ultimately rule higher correlations. It is crucial to note that the overall number of edges is not fixed in this ansatz, only the network size N is held constant.

4.1.1 Configuration Model Scheme

Bearing in mind the required properties the mutation scheme must obey, it is a promising ansatz to induce some variations in the degree sequence within a given network realization. The idea is to apply the configuration model (CM) algorithm, which is used to generate uncorrelated networks with an a priori fixed degree distribution $P(k)$, to a small fraction of a network. The algorithm used to generate a whole network assigns each vertex a degree which is sampled from the desired degree distribution $P(k)$. Then these drawn degrees of each vertex are converted into a discrete representation of the corresponding edge end distribution $P_e(k)$ by building up a list which includes for each vertex i exactly k_i entries. Here k_i is the degree of vertex i and the entries for vertex i within the list represent open edge ends bound to vertex i. Edges are then created by joining two edge ends sampled successively from that list. The CM mutation scheme is motivated by the former algorithm and defined as follows:

1. Initially a fraction of n nodes is randomly selected from the current network to be mutated.

2. For every selected vertex i, a new target degree $\tilde{k}_i$ is sampled from the degree distribution $P(k)$ of the *current* network realization.

3. The selected vertices are successively processed in order to remove the edges which start from each vertex i. However, a random amount of edges, drawn from the range $[0, \min\{k_i, \tilde{k}_i\}]$, is not deleted. The difference among the target degree $\tilde{k}_i$ and the number of edges kept yields the number of open edge ends to be joined for vertex i within the next steps. In removing an edge from vertex i the adjacent vertex, which is connected by this edge to vertex i, will loose an edge end. If the connected vertex is not in the set of selected vertices, this loss must be compensated by assigning an open edge end to a randomly chosen vertex in the network.

4. All open edge ends are collected in a list which contains as many entries for each vertex as there are open edge ends for that particular vertex.

4 Evolution of Networks

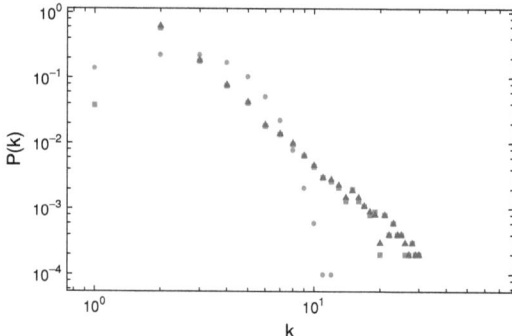

Figure 4.1: Degree distribution $P(k)$ of the initial (circles), target (triangle) and final (square) networks which were mutated with the CM mutation scheme.

5. Finally, edges are assembled by consecutively drawing pairs from the open edge end list. Once an edge is formed, the respective edge ends are removed from the list. This is repeated until the list is empty.

In step two the scheme utilizes apparently an information from the full network, the current degree distribution $P(k)$, to randomly assign new degrees to vertices. The removal of the edges emanating from the set of selected vertices is quite involved. The possibility to guard some edges helps to maintain possible correlations. The actual removal of an edge which leads to a vertex which is not in the set of selected vertices must be balanced by the assignment of an open edge end. This assignment is necessarily made to a random vertex within the network and not to the vertex which looses the edge end. Otherwise, the network would be bound to the set of degrees it initially had, since all other degrees would have a weight of 0 for all mutations due to the sampling with respect to the current degree distribution. By construction of the scheme, the degree distribution will be maintained on average if no selection mechanism is used. Only small variations of the network with respect to the degree distribution are successively generated.

Since the CM mutation scheme is closely related to the CM procedure used to generate uncorrelated networks of arbitrary degree distribution $P(k)$, it is expected that the CM mutation scheme is capable to successfully mutate the degree sequence of an arbitrary initial network realization into the direction of an arbitrary different degree distribution. Exploiting the testing scheme introduced above confirms this expectation. Figure 4.1 shows the evaluation of the CM mutation scheme with an

4.1 Network Mutation

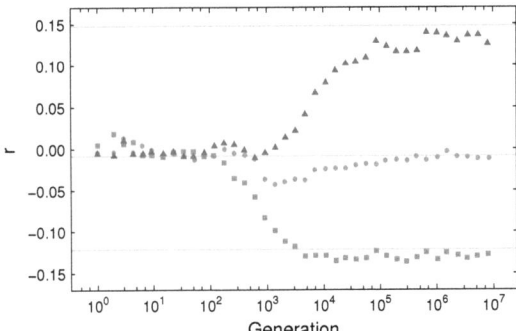

Figure 4.2: Newman factor r during the evaluation of the CM mutation scheme. Reference lines are drawn for the Newman factor r of the target networks which have assortative (triangle), uncorrelated (square), or disassortative (circle) two-point correlations.

initially Erdős-Rényi type network and an uncorrelated scale-free network with a scaling exponent $\gamma = 3$ as the target topology. The network size has been set to $N = 10^3$, the fraction of vertices selected in each mutation step is 1%, and the results are averaged over 10 independent runs. While the initial network (circle) has a Poissonian degree distribution, vastly different from a power-law form of the target network (triangle), the mutation scheme achieves an almost precise match (square) with the target degree distribution. A single exception can be observed for vertices with degree 1. Such vertices are not present in the target network, but have a high frequency within the initial network. In the final network obtained the frequency of degree 1 vertices is decreased. This decline continues with longer runs and the frequency would vanish for extremely long runs.

However, while the uncorrelated case is expected to work well, the build up of two-point correlations should be difficult to attain. Even though some pre-cautions have been undertaken to allow for the build up of correlations, the CM scheme is exclusively used to generate uncorrelated networks since only the degree distribution $P(k)$ is taken into account. Even though higher correlations are ignored by the CM mutation scheme, the procedure is capable to reproduce two-point correlations within the testing scheme. Repeating the evaluation with scale-free networks reveals a good achievement with targeted two-point correlations set to assortative (triangle), uncorrelated (square), and disassortative (circle) as shown in Fig. 4.2. In difference

4 Evolution of Networks

to the network used above, the correlation parameter α has been set to 0.4 (-0.4) for the (diss-)assortative networks. The curves for two-point correlated cases both show a slight offset below the target Newman values. This shift originates in the difficulty arising from vertices with degree 1. While these vertices are not present in the target network, they are still present in the mutated network and cause a slight shift towards disassortative correlations.

4.1.2 Copying Scheme

Replication is one of natures primary driving forces. Applying this idea onto the context of a network mutation is evidently not comparable to some biological replication scheme even though such connection can be made [Evlampiev & Isambert, 2008]. However, the concept of copying larger objects is an appealing approach, since this offers the possibility to amplify distinct correlation patterns of higher order. A characteristic the former CM mutation scheme lacks. Translating this concept to a mutation procedure leads to the copy mutation scheme:

1. From the network under mutation a fraction of n nodes is randomly drawn. These nodes will be copied within the next steps and are referred to as source vertices. The random sampling is done successively to label each vertex with an integer. Additionally the degree k_i of each source vertex i is saved.

2. The same fraction of n nodes is randomly chosen from the remaining set of vertices. These are the target vertices and are labeled as well with an integer. All edges of the target vertices are removed. Within this removal the degree of a source vertex might become decreased which is why the degree of each source vertex has been saved in the previous step.

3. The source set of vertices is now consecutively iterated. Starting with the first vertex sampled in step one all edges of this vertex are copied onto the first vertex from the target set. If an edge from the source vertex points to a vertex which is not in the source set, then the vertex from the target set will be connected to that vertex. If on the other hand an edge from the source vertex is connected to another vertex which is a source vertex as well, then the target vertex will gain a connection with the corresponding vertex in the target set. The correspondence is established by the labeling performed in the former two steps. This scheme is repeated for all source vertices until all edges from the source set are copied to the target set.

4. Within the removal of all edges in step two some source vertices have possibly lost some edges. These edges are missing within the source set and are as well absent in the target set since they did not get copied. This is compensated for

4.1 Network Mutation

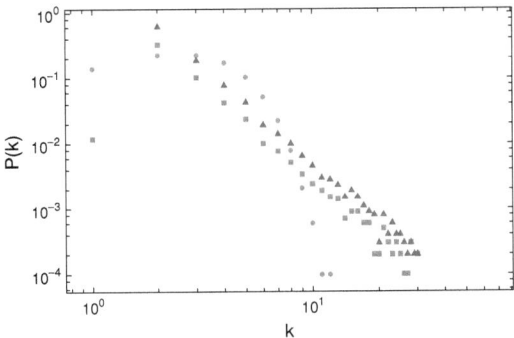

Figure 4.3: Degree distribution $P(k)$ of the initial (circle), target (triangle) and final (square) networks which were mutated with the copy mutation scheme.

by adding the lost edges again. A vertex from the source set with lost edges is assigned the missing amount of edges. The edges are connected to random vertices from the target set.

The copy mutation scheme must take into account the fixed system size N of the network to mutate such that a target set of vertices onto which in each step the scheme copies the source vertices must be determined. All connections from the target set are removed while extra care must be undertaken for edges connecting the source and the target set of vertices. Once the edges from the target set are removed, the information about these edges is lost within the copying step. Therefore, the degree of each source vertex is recorded just before the removal of the edges from the target vertices set. Redistributing these special edges in step four assures that on average the total number of edges in the network does not change if no selection mechanism is applied. The reassignment of these special edges in step four is realized by a random scheme to gain some variations within the degree sequence of the network.

The results of a first test whether the copy mutation scheme is capable to attain an arbitrary degree distribution with the evaluation method formerly introduced is shown in Fig. 4.3. The initial network is again an Erdős-Rényi network (circle) with a Poisson degree distribution while the target topology (triangle) is a scale-free degree distribution $P(k)$ with a scaling exponent $\gamma = 3$. Two-point correlations are absent within the target network. The final network (square) after overall 10^7 mutation steps displays a power-law degree distribution $P(k)$ for nodes with degrees

4 Evolution of Networks

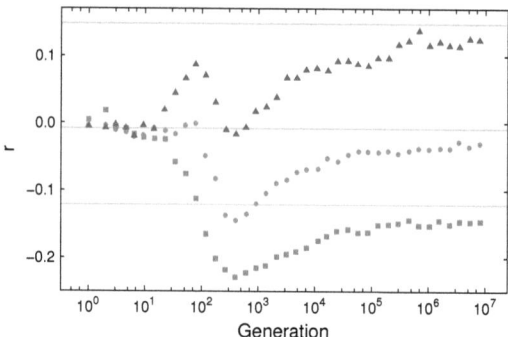

Figure 4.4: Newman factor r during the evaluation of the copy mutation scheme. Symbols and reference lines correspond to Fig. 4.2.

larger than 1 which can be well approximated with a scaling exponent of the target topology. The major difference is the systematic offset of the resulting final degree distribution towards lower frequencies. This shift is reflected by a considerably decreased average degree $\bar{k}$. While the initial average degree is 3.03, the final average degree is 1.64. It turns out that this decrease in the average degree results from a higher acceptance probability of the applied selection criteria if a mutation occurs which lowers the average degree. Supposing a mutation step which increases the average degree, it is very likely that a vertex with a large degree is involved. Copying such a large degree vertex has a significant impact on the scoring function. However, simply by the large amount of edges copied it is very likely that correlations are copied which oppose the targets topological properties. As a result the probability is higher for a rejection of mutation steps involving vertices with a large degree.

In Fig. 4.4 results are shown for the extended evaluation tests with correlated networks. The same parameter set has been used as in the previous section for the CM mutation scheme. The copy mutation scheme is able to reproduce the correlations of the target topology. The curves first fall into the disassortative regime and then converge into the direction of the target value of the Newman factor r. The trend of all three curves suggests for a longer duration the convergence onto the correct final value of the Newman coefficient. The pronounced shift towards disassortative values of the Newman factor r in comparison to the CM scheme roots back in the relatively increased frequency of vertices of degree 1. This is observable from a comparison of the final histograms of the copy and the CM mutation scheme in Fig. 4.3 and Fig. 4.1, respectively. Lowering the frequency of degree 1 vertices is for both schemes difficult and is slightly pronounced in the copy scheme. The increased frequency of vertices with degree 1 is responsible for the shift towards disassortative two-point correlations.

The observed decrease of the average degree could be interpreted as a drawback of the copy mutation scheme. The cause is an increased rejection probability for mutations which include large degree vertices. In spite of the inaccuracies caused within the evaluation tests, this behavior is of great advantage in an evolution driven by dynamics. Evidently, the rejected mutations have a large impact on the network topology. Therefore, the copy mutation scheme is able to generate mutated networks with a significant topology change.

4.2 Network Selection by Dynamics

The selection process is a major cornerstone of an evolution. A common ansatz is to model the evolutionary process in a framework of successively evolving finite populations. The Moran process is an elementary stochastic model to study selection acting on a finite population of distinct individuals. The process considers a population of fixed size which evolves in discrete generations. Within each generation a random individual for reproduction and a random individual for death is selected. Therefore, the offspring of the former individual replaces the latter which is why the process is also referred to as birth-death model. The initial population in the first generation is assumed to consist out of different types of individuals. Supposing there are only two types i and j of individuals available initially and supposing a perfect reproduction without mutation, then the process has two absorbing states. Once either type becomes extinct, the population will stay for all subsequent generations homogeneous. This event is called the fixation of a certain type. The probability for such an event to occur given a particular generation is referred to as fixation probability.

Turning back to the context of evolution where mutations at a rate μ within reproduction steps are possible, a formerly homogeneous population of a particular type i can give birth to a single mutant type j. This situation of a large and almost homogeneous population of type i, called the wild-type, and a mutant type j is a common scenario within biology. At what probability the mutant type j can create a lineage which takes over the whole population is given by the fixation probability $P(i \to j)$. If all individuals are selected with the same probability in each step for a reproduction or a death event, then the fixation probability is $1/N_\mathrm{p}$. This changes in the presence of fitness criteria. The fitness is interpretable in a biological setting

4 Evolution of Networks

as the adaptability to the given environment of an individual. A higher fitness than other individuals ultimately means a higher reproduction rate. Coining this onto the Moran process translates into a preferential selection of individuals with a higher fitness for reproduction events. Assuming a fitness of f_j for a single mutant j arising in a population of wild-type i with fitness f_i, the fixation probability is

$$P(i \to j) = \frac{1 - \frac{f_i}{f_j}}{1 - \left(\frac{f_i}{f_j}\right)^{N_p}}. \tag{4.2}$$

Evaluating this fixation probability for mutants which have a fitness advantage over the wild-type, i.e. $f_j > f_i$, reveals that a higher fitness does not necessarily guarantee to replace the population. In addition it is even possible within finite populations for mutants with a decreased fitness to take over the population.

The evolutionary process can be mapped onto a Markov process [Sella & Hirsh, 2005]. By the structure of the Markov process a stationary state will be reached. The distribution of states within the stationary regime have been shown by Sella & Hirsh [2005] to be Boltzmann distributed. This allows for the description of the stationary state in terms of a canonical ensemble in equilibrium from thermodynamics. A translation of the evolutionary variables can be established by identifying the negative logarithmic fitness $-\ln f$ as energy E and the population size N_p as inverse temperature β.

The evolution carried out in this Thesis aims at identifying the optimal topologies of a network with respect to the dynamical processes considered here. These optimal structures emerge in the course of an evolution and are realized in the stationary state. In this sense, a standard Monte-Carlo scheme [Binder & Heermann, 1997] with Boltzmann weights is applicable to perform the network selection process, which is implemented by:

1. Initially a single Erdős-Rényi graph is created and the largest component is extracted from the graph. This graph forms the initial network for the evolution.

2. The fitness of the network $-\ln f_i$ is measured by running the dynamical process in question on the network. The fitness measure is a scalar value and depends on the particular dynamical process. The value of the fitness measure is commonly averaged over multiple runs of the dynamics on the same network to obtain its mean value.

3. The network is mutated with the CM or the copy mutation scheme. Only mutations which maintain the largest component are permitted. If the network disintegrates into multiple components, the mutation is rejected and repeated with the original network.

4.2 Network Selection by Dynamics

4. The fitness of the mutated network $-\ln f_j$ is observed as in step two. The mutated network replaces the former network if the negative logarithm is lower than that of the current network or if a randomly sampled number s in the range of $[0, 1]$ fulfills the condition

$$s < \exp\left[-\beta \left(\ln f_i - \ln f_j\right)\right], \quad (4.3)$$

where the parameter β is the inverse temperature. In case the mutated network is discarded, the former network is recovered.

5. Steps three and four are successively iterated for a sufficiently large amount of generations.

6. Finally, the full network structure is saved.

The evolution requires some pre-cautions to consider. For example, the network must be fully connected in the course of the evolution. This is ensured within step three which immediately rejects any mutation leading to a defragmented network. Recalling Eq. (2.13) in Sec. 2.2 reveals that this restricts admissible degree sequences to comply with the condition of Eq. (2.13), $\overline{k^2} > 2\overline{k}$.

A further peculiarity of the scheme is the a priori unknown inverse temperature β which constrains the acceptance rate. The common method to perform such an optimization at temperature 0 leads to vanishing acceptance rates in the cases studied. To ensure a sufficiently high acceptance rate, the inverse temperature is tuned by the algorithm such that a pre-defined acceptance rate r is attained. Initially β is set to an appropriate value and an increment factor $\hat{\beta}$ is fixed. The inverse temperature is multiplied with the increment factor $\hat{\beta}$ each time a mutant network is accepted which lowers the temperature. If a mutant network is discarded, the inverse temperature is lowered by multiplying β with

$$\tilde{\beta} = \hat{\beta}^{\frac{r}{r-1}}. \quad (4.4)$$

With this choice, the inverse temperature will remain at a constant value, once the acceptance rate r is reached. The acceptance rate is set to $r = 0.2$ and the increment factor $\hat{\beta}$ is equals to 1.01 within the evolutions considered here.

The results obtained with this evolution scheme are averaged over multiple different initial realizations of the starting Erdős-Rényi network with an average degree of $\overline{k} = 6$ to observe the mean behavior. In addition, a crosscheck with a regular three-dimensional lattice as initial network is performed to assure the independence of the results from initial network topology. In the course of the evolution only one network realization and one mutant network is in each generation considered, even though evolution regulates the development of a population. However, this setting

4 Evolution of Networks

corresponds to a wide spread observed situation in biology that the population size N_p is large while the mutation rate μ is low, such that

$$\mu N_\text{p} \ll 1 \tag{4.5}$$

is valid. In this limit, there are at maximum two different types of individuals present in each instant within a population. Effectively the population can be represented by a single individual and a mutant replaces that individual with a probability given by the fixation probability.

4.2.1 Reaction-Diffusion Process

Driving an evolution by a selection mechanism based on the diffusion-annihilation reaction $A + B \to \emptyset$ requires a thorough choice of the initial parameters. The networks considered here within the context of the diffusion-annihilation dynamics have a size of $N = 10^3$. This size is comparable to many biological networks. The limited network size constraints consequently the smallest density which is resolvable. Dynamical states which have a particle density close to the minimal density $\rho_\text{min} = 2/N$ will certainly not reflect the typical system behavior. Running an annihilation reaction until all particles are vanished will display strong finite-size effects, such that the density until which the process is considered is limited to $2\rho_\text{min}$. While the final density is limited to avoid finite-size effects, the initial density must be limited as well. Starting of with a fully occupied network would emphasize the deterministic characteristics of the diffusion-annihilation dynamics and neglect topological differences. However, with decreasing initial density the reaction will run shorter, having strong fluctuations within any fitness measure as consequence. A choice of $\rho_0 = 0.1$ will be used for the following. This initial density balances the aspects raised.

A crucial ingredient for the evolution driven by a dynamics is the used fitness measure. This measure ultimately defines which type of topology the evolution will select. Consequently, a trivial fitness measure has a trivial topology as its solution. An apparent fitness measure is the speed of the reaction. The time elapsed t_f scales with the number of particles which annihilate, such that a normalization by the number of annihilation events

$$-\ln f^\text{S} = \frac{t_f}{2 \text{ total \# annihilations}} \tag{4.6}$$

yields the average annihilation duration per particle. Assuring a fast reaction rate and maximising the speed of the overall density decay will minimize f^S. A requirement for an annihilation event to occur is the existence of an AB contact. The

4.2 Network Selection by Dynamics

optimal solution for this problem is evidently a star graph with one central node which has the degree $k = N - 1$ and $N - 1$ further nodes of degree $k = 1$. This structure is fully connected as required by the connectedness constraint and enforces the strongest possible mixing among the particles.

Performing an evolution with both mutation schemes with respect to this speed fitness measure confirms these considerations. The copy mutation scheme is capable to recover the star topology. In contrast, the CM mutation scheme fails to drive the network into a star topology. The CM mutation scheme is incapable to substantially alter the topology of the initial network and the resulting values for the speed fitness measure f^S are smaller than results for the copy mutation scheme. This roots in the inability of the CM scheme to generate network mutations which are substantially different than the original network. The mutant networks are indifferent from the point view of the dynamics with respect to the speed measure introduced in Eq. (4.6).

Aside of reaction speed, the diffusion-annihilation shows pattern formation. The measures Q_{AB} and P_{AB} introduced in Sec. 3.1.3 capture in essence pattern formation, but are not directly applicable within their form defined. Both observables are defined in each instant of the reaction and do not characterize the overall dynamical process by a scalar value. Recalling the definition of the efficiency measure P_{AB}, which measures the annihilation rate in ratio to the rate of created AB contacts, leads to an efficiency measure characteristic for the whole reaction. Defining an efficiency measure as

$$-\ln f^P = \frac{\text{total \# annihilations}}{\text{total \# created } AB \text{ contacts}} \quad (4.7)$$

yields a scalar value suitable to be used as an effectivity fitness measure. The most efficient reaction possible will need only one created AB contact per annihilation such that the the largest value possible of the rhs from Eq. (4.7) is exactly 1. Lower values indicate a decreased efficiency. This fitness measures requires consequently the separation of the two reactants until they react. The optimal structure to fulfill this criteria is a one-dimensional chain. Within such a structure mixed regions will extremely fast segregate and each AB contact will result with a probability of $1/2$ into an annihilation event. Structures which support a high level of segregation are therefore favourable with respect to the efficiency measure. Lattices with low dimensions beneath the critical dimension 4 fulfill this condition in general. However, performed evolution runs are not capable to find these structures. By the nature of the random sampling process structures as lattices, which are highly regular, are very unlikely to be found by the random schemes applied here.

Both measures introduced favour vastly different topologies. While the solution to efficiency fitness measure is in terms of the degree distribution a delta functional

4 Evolution of Networks

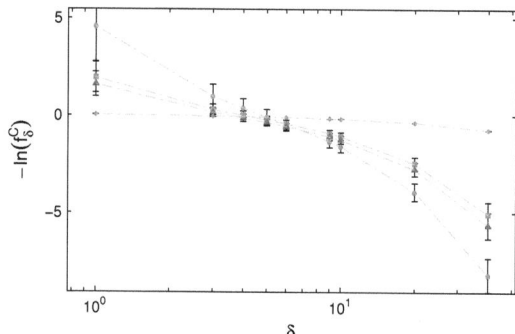

Figure 4.5: The mean logarithmic combined fitness measure $\ln f_\delta^C$ of the annihilation reaction is shown for different weighting of the evolutionary targets speed and efficiency. The bars indicate the standard deviations and the topologies exemplifies are a star (diamond), two-dimensional periodic lattice (circle), an Erdős-Rényi graph with average degree $\bar{k} = 6$ (square), and an uncorrelated scale-free network (triangle) with scaling exponent $\gamma = 2.75$.

at degree $k = 1$, the other speed measure will lead to a a degree distribution which has a weight of $N - 1$ at degree $k = 1$ and weight 1 for degree $k = N - 1$. A promising approach is the combination of these contrary evolutionary targets into a combined fitness measure. The necessity to optimize two contrary evolutionary targets at the same time is characteristic for biological systems. In order to weight which of the two targets are to be optimized, a weighting parameter δ is introduced. The resulting energies in units of $k_\mathrm{B}T$ used for the Monte-Carlo scheme are

$$-\ln f_\delta^C = -\delta \ln f^S - \frac{1}{\delta} \ln f^P. \qquad (4.8)$$

Evaluating this combined fitness measure for the topologies considered so far is shown in Fig. 4.5. The fitness measure f_δ^C is evaluated for different values of δ on the topological structures of a star (diamond), a periodic two-dimensional lattice (circle), and an uncorrelated scale-free network (triangle) with a scaling exponent $\gamma = 2.75$. The one-dimensional chain has been omitted since it has such a slow reaction speed that it is out of scope from the region plotted. The resulting energies as defined by Eq. (4.8) are drawn vs. the weighting parameter δ along with the respective standard deviations which are indicated by the bars in each direction.

4.2 Network Selection by Dynamics

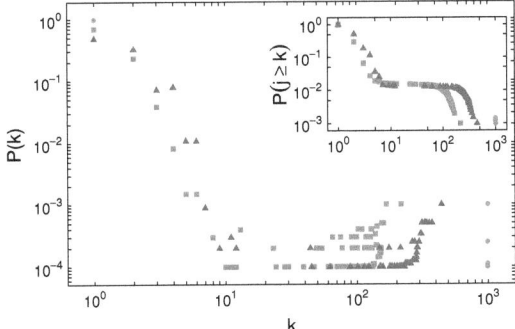

Figure 4.6: Final degree distribution $P(k)$ of an evolution with copy mutation scheme driven by selection based on the process $A + B \to \emptyset$. The distributions shown are for the values δ equals to 1 (circle), 3 (triangle), and 10 (square). As an inset the cumulative degree distributions $P(j \geq k)$ are illustrated.

For values of δ in the vicinity of 1, the star topology has the lowest value with a standard deviation close to 0. With increasing values of δ, the advantage of the star disappears as the other curves attain lower values. With a value of approximately $\delta = 5$, the star is not any longer the best topology. At this value of the weighting parameter δ the topology becomes indifferent with respect to the fitness criteria as all curves fall onto a single point. Shortly after this crossing point, the curves suggest a slight advantage of the scale-free topology, but no clear distinction can be made since the standard deviations are too large. With increasing values of the weighting factor δ, the periodic two-dimensional lattice becomes again the optimal topological structure.

These observations make an evolution of the diffusion-annihilation appear very difficult. The outcome of three evolutions with the values of δ equals to 1 (circle), 3 (triangle), and 10 (square) is shown in Fig. 4.6. All data-points have been averaged over 10 independent evolutions for each value of δ. The copy mutation scheme is used within all shown evolutions. Evolutions under the the CM mutation scheme have shown to be incapable to optimize the fitness criteria for reasons explained above. The degree distributions, illustrated in Fig. 4.6, show no apparent functional form. Solely the degree distribution $P(k)$ corresponding to the evolution, which effectively optimizes for speed, is characteristic for a star like topology. Almost all vertices

4 Evolution of Networks

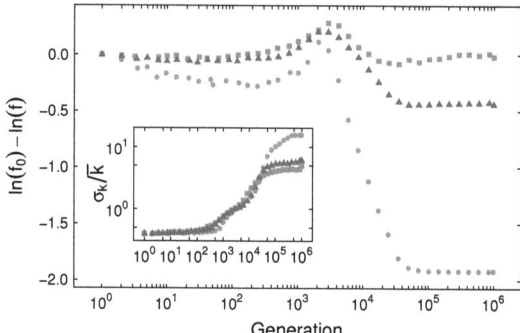

Figure 4.7: Fitness during an evolution of the $A + B \to \emptyset$ process with different weights δ for the evolutionary target. The inset shows the variability of the degree sequence. The symbols correspond to Fig. 4.6.

have degree 1 while only a few vertices have a degree which is of the order of the system size $N = 10^3$. The other two degree distributions follow for a small range a power-law, but outside this range the degree distribution can not be captured by some common functional form. The respective curves of the combined fitness is shown Fig. 4.7. The initial values have been subtracted for comparability such that all curves start at 0. Apparently, the evolution is able to optimize the fitness measure for a value of $\delta = 1$, which corresponds to a star, much better than for the other evolutions with larger values of δ. The inset in Fig. 4.7 shows the variability of the degree sequence which is measured in terms of the standard deviation σ_k in relation to the mean degree $\overline{k}$,

$$\frac{\sigma_k}{\overline{k}} = \frac{\sqrt{\overline{k^2} - \overline{k}^2}}{\overline{k}}. \tag{4.9}$$

The variability increases dramatically within every evolutionary run and attains a constant level as final value. The star topology for the $\delta = 1$ evolution evidently has the highest variability while the other two evolutions have a decreased variability in comparison. Nevertheless, the variability for the $\delta = 3$ and $\delta = 10$ are considerably high as they are well above 1.

A tabular comparison of the final fitness values is shown in Tab. 4.1. The data shows the obtained fitness values by the evolution along with fitness values from the presented topologies above for the three values of the parameter δ considered

4.2 Network Selection by Dynamics

Topology	Mean fitness	Std. Dev.	δ
Erdős-Rényi	0.03	0.01	1
Star	0.03	0.01	1
Scale-Free	1.59	0.62	1
2D lattice	1.93	0.78	1
Evolution	4.57	1.82	1
Erdős-Rényi	-0.14	0.03	3
Star	-0.04	0.00	3
Scale-Free	0.15	0.23	3
2D lattice	0.30	0.28	3
Evolution	0.97	0.62	3
Evolution	-1.59	0.31	10
Scale-Free	-1.25	0.19	10
Erdős-Rényi	-1.10	0.15	10
2D lattice	-1.07	0.19	10
Star	-0.18	0.00	10

Table 4.1: Average combined fitness $-\ln f_\delta^C$ for different topologies and values of the weighting parameter δ.

here. The network topologies found by the evolution are in case of the parameter δ being in the range which favors the speed fitness criteria within the range of the optimal topology as predicted above. For the large values of the parameter $\delta = 10$, the fitness measure favours highly regular topologies. These are inaccessible to the random sampling scheme used here such that the evolution is not able to find a topology which is better than the two-dimensional lattice.

4.2.2 Prisoner's Dilemma

The Prisoner's Dilemma arises from the question how cooperation can sustain such that an apparent fitness criteria for the dynamics is based on the cooperator density ρ,

$$-\ln f^\rho = -\rho. \tag{4.10}$$

This guides the evolution to select topologies with a high level of cooperation ρ. This level of cooperation is constrained by the single parameter of the dynamics, the temptation to defect b. An evolution is consequently performed at an *a priori* fixed value of b. The choice of this parameter is important, since the initial conformation of the network is an Erdős-Rényi when the evolution is started. This structure supports

4 Evolution of Networks

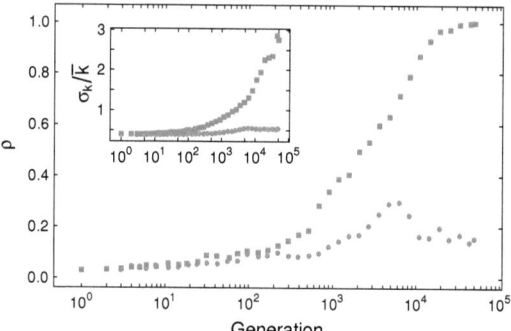

Figure 4.8: Plot shows the cooperator density ρ during an evolution of the Prisoner's Dilemma dynamics at a temptation to defect of $b = 1.6$. The symbols indicate the different mutation schemes used, CM (circle) and copy (square). The inset shows the variability of the degree sequence.

only marginally the sustainment of cooperation such that cooperator densities are very low. However, the cooperator density has to be larger than the minimal density resolvable by the given system size N. Otherwise the evolution would not see any cooperation at all, just by a too small system size.

Recalling that the Prisoner's Dilemma has a stationary state within which the cooperator density ρ is assumed to be stable, it is hence necessary to drive the dynamics through the transient phase for each candidate network in the course an evolution. The stationarity has the convenient side effect that the cooperator density is not subject to strong fluctuations. This allows for a low number of statistics per network candidate which were set to 10 dynamical runs per network tried. The downside of the stationarity is the much increased computational resources required. For that reason the system size has been set to a value of $N = 500$ which is still a realistic network size in terms of biological networks which are subject to cooperation.

The efficiency version of the Prisoner's Dilemma turns out to be very hard to optimize. Neither the CM nor the copy scheme are capable to improve the cooperation level. A problem in this case are the extremely low cooperator densities at the evaluated temptation to defect b of 1.6. Decreasing the temptation to defect b to lower values as 1.3 improves this, but does not solve the problem of marginal cooperation density. A decreasment of the temptation to defect parameter b to values as low as 1.05 assures that the cooperators are able to spread over the whole network, since

4.2 Network Selection by Dynamics

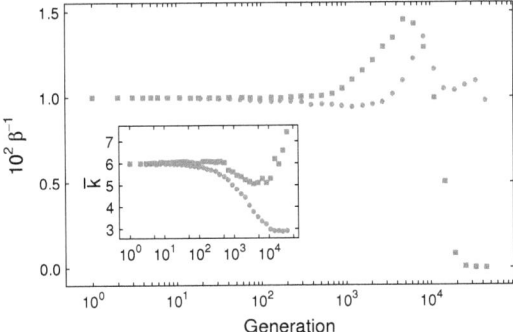

Figure 4.9: Temperature β^{-1} in the course of an evolution of the accumulated Prisoner's Dilemma game at a temptation to defect of $b = 1.6$. The inset shows the mean degree $\bar{k}$ during the evolution.

the cooperator strategy is in the ESS_N class for all vertices, including the vertices with the largest degree $k_{\max}$, see Sec. 3.2. This choice in turn does not leave much room for fitness gains. The cooperator density ρ is at this level of the temptation to defect parameter $b \approx 1$ already close to 1. The evolution based on a CM mutation scheme maintains the level of cooperation which is initially present. The CM scheme does not alter the topology of the underlying network, the changes induced by the CM scheme are too small to be sensed by the dynamics which is in accordance with the diffusion-annihilation reaction. On the other hand, the copy scheme generates in the course of an evolution some mutant networks which display large fluctuations within the cooperator density. The selection scheme follows, once these fluctuations are too large, only the noise from the fitness measure. As a result the cooperator density is decreased.

The situation is different in the accumulated Prisoner's Dilemma dynamics. To some extent it is evident for the evolution which topological changes improve the level of cooperation. Nodes with a large degree k help to maintain a high level of cooperation, since the vertices are inert against strategy adaption. In contrast to that, a low mean degree $\bar{k}$ increases the density of cooperation which is supported by observations drawn from an increasing average degree $\bar{k}$ for Erdős-Rényi networks in Sec. 3.2 along with a decreasing cooperator density. A large mean degree $\bar{k}$ implies pronounced mean-field behavior which corresponds to the absence of cooperation. Both topological changes appear to be incompatible to one another and it is not

4 Evolution of Networks

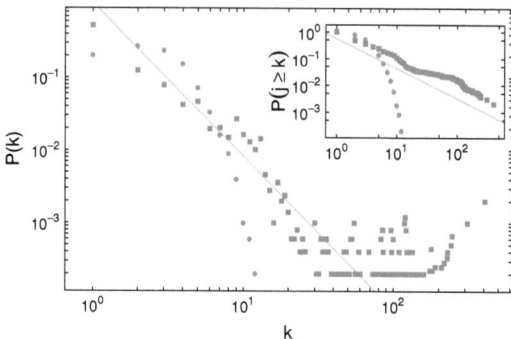

Figure 4.10: Degree distribution of networks from an evolution with respect to the cooperator density of the Prisoner's Dilemma. The mutation schemes used are the CM (circle) and the copy (square) scheme. The inset shows the cumulative degree distribution $P(j \geq k)$ where a scaling exponent $\gamma = 2.11$ has been determined and drawn as a reference line within both figures.

obvious what type of topology will emerge within an evolution. The density of cooperators ρ is shown in Fig. 4.8 for an evolution performed at a temptation to defect $b = 1.6$ with the CM (circle) and copy (square) mutation scheme. While the copy scheme successfully optimizes the density of cooperation to its maximal value of 1, the CM (circle) scheme is not able to overcome a certain level of cooperation. A key ingredient of the copy (circle) mutation scheme to increase the cooperation density is the increase of the variability of the degree sequence which is shown as an inset in Fig. 4.8. Surprisingly, the CM scheme shows a slight decline in the cooperator density ρ at a generation of roughly 10^4. At this point the acceptance rate decreases significantly which is indicated by the increasing temperature, illustrated in Fig. 4.9. This roots in the continuous reduction of the mean degree $\overline{k}$ by the CM scheme. The mean degree $\overline{k}$, shown as an inset in Fig. 4.9, is lowered to a value of $\overline{k} = 2.87$. A further reduction of the mean degree $\overline{k}$ is impossible, since the network has to stay fully connected. The final degree distributions $P(k)$ are shown in Fig. 4.10. Evidently, the CM scheme keeps the functional form of the initial Poisson degree distribution and only pushes the initial mean degree $\overline{k} = 6$ to a lower value. The results from the copy scheme are vastly different. Evaluating the degree distribution by cumulative statistics, which is shown as an inset in Fig. 4.10, reveals that the final functional form is compatible with a power-law fit. This suggests that a scale-free degree distribution is indeed an optimal structure for the support of cooperation within the accumulated Prisoner's Dilemma dynamics. A least-squares fit of the cumulative degree distribution estimates a scaling exponent γ of 2.11. The lines drawn within the double logarithmic plots of Fig. 4.10 have the respective slopes and are well compatible with the data.

4.3 Conclusion

The influence of a dynamical process has been studied in the framework of evolution. Two network mutation schemes were introduced. The configuration model (CM) mutation scheme considered is motivated by the CM scheme to construct uncorrelated networks. It focuses on the degree distribution of a network, producing mutant networks which have a similar degree distribution as the original network but include some variations. The other mutation scheme was based on the principle of copying. A fraction of vertices from the original network is copied with all edges among these vertices onto a random target region of the network. Both schemes were thoroughly evaluated whether they allow for an ergodic sampling of the network ensemble. The CM and the copy mutation scheme were verified to fulfill this requirement within the testing scheme applied. However, the testing revealed a minor short-coming of the copy scheme which slightly decreases the average degree $\overline{k}$ in the course of the test performed. The reduction of the average degree $\overline{k}$ is due to a large impact on the network topology whenever the copy mutation scheme processes vertices with a large degree k in a mutation step. Such mutation steps with a large impact on the network topology are in the majority of cases opposing to the two-point correlations found in the target network. Therefore, mutations which involve such large degree vertices have a higher probability of being rejected.

The reduction of the average degree $\overline{k}$ may appear at a first glance disadvantageous and disqualify it as a proper mutation scheme. However, further tests reveal that if no selection criteria is applied, the average degree $\overline{k}$ remains constant. The large topological changes, which occur whenever a vertex of large degree k is copied, are a hindrance in the tests performed, but will turn out to help an evolution to explore topologies which substantially deviate from the initial topology.

Key concept of an evolution is the selection method. The final stationary distribution defined by a biological evolution like the Moran process is Boltzmann distributed [Sella & Hirsh, 2005]. As the focus here is on the final stationary state, the selection method has been realized by means of a Monte-Carlo sampling scheme with Boltzmann weights. The energies minimized by the Monte-Carlo scheme correspond to the negative logarithm of the fitness measure used, as shown in Sella & Hirsh [2005]. The fitness measure of a network is a scalar value defined by an appropriate observable from the dynamics performed on the network.

In the case of the reaction-diffusion process, $A + B \to \emptyset$, the choice of the fitness measure turned out to be difficult. Choosing reaction speed as a fitness measure results in the trivial topology of a star. In contrast, the efficiency measure leads to a further trivial structure of a regular lattice. The two fitness measures were combined with the help of a weighting parameter which controls to what extent one or the other fitness measure is used. Evaluating this combined fitness measure shows that either a trivial topology is optimal or the fitness measure is indifferent with respect to random network topologies as different as scale-free and Erdős-Rényi type networks. The performed evolutions with the copy mutation scheme confirm the expectation to obtain one of the trivial structures. The evolutions with the CM mutation scheme, on the contrary, failed to optimize any fitness measure. This failure roots in the inability of the CM mutation scheme to generate mutant networks which have significant topological changes causing an impact on the fitness measure. In summary, the diffusion-annihilation process appears to be very difficult to use to study network evolution driven by selection on dynamics. The observations suggest that a meaningful evolution requires the existence of a stationary state of the dynamics like it is common in biological systems.

The Prisoner's Dilemma is free from the drawback of lacking a stationary state as the $A + B \to \emptyset$ reaction. The density of cooperators in the stationary state of the Prisoner's Dilemma is used as a fitness measure. The temptation to defect parameter b constrains the density of cooperation and its value is a priori fixed in the course of an evolution. The two versions of the Prisoner's Dilemma considered here have vastly different dynamical properties, which is reflected in the evolution of these.

The effective payoff version of the dynamics reveals either to be insensitive against topological changes induced by the mutation schemes or is subject to large fluctuations. The behavior of the efficiency ruled dynamics is characterized to be almost unaware of the underlying network topology. The insensitivity roots back in the rules of the dynamics, since the transformation of payoffs into effective payoffs virtually removes the topological fingerprint from the dynamical process. This is in accordance with the proposed equivalence in Sec. 3.2 that each vertex within the network is representable by a player who is playing the Prisoner's Dilemma in a population of size k, the degree of the vertex. The efficiency ruled dynamics consequently ignores to a large extent the network structure.

The situation changes drastically in the case of accumulated payoffs. The accumulation procedure ensures the direct impact of the topology on the dynamics. The accumulated dynamics leads to different network topologies under the evolution with the two mutation schemes. At a temptation to defect value of $b = 1.6$, the copy mutation scheme is capable to optimize the cooperator density to the highest possible value $\rho = 1$, while the CM mutation scheme attains a cooperator density considerably smaller. The CM mutation scheme is not capable to generate topological changes which simultaneously deviate from the initial Erdős-Rényi network topology and induce a significant impact on the fitness measure of the cooperator density. Instead, the CM mutation scheme keeps the Poisson degree distribution of the initial network and reduces the mean degree $\overline{k}$. The reduction of the average degree $\overline{k}$ is a convenient method to increase the cooperator density. This moves the system further away from a mean-field scenario which corresponds to an all-to-all interaction pattern, where cooperation is absent. However, reducing the average degree $\overline{k}$ is only possible to some extent as the network is required to stay connected. The CM mutation scheme does not explore the inertness of vertices with a large degree. Such vertices with a large degree stabilize cooperation significantly. The copy mutation scheme manages to build up vertices with a large degree. In the course of an evolution, the copy mutation constantly increases the variability of the degree distribution which is crucial for the support of the inertness by vertices with a large degree. The obtained degree distribution is compatible with a power-law, suggesting that a scale-free network topology is indeed optimal with respect to the accumulated Prisoner's Dilemma.

5 Conclusion and Discussion

The onset of this Thesis was the development of an analytical framework which allows to control the studied topological properties. The result has been a general formalism capable to control two-point correlations on the level of the average nearest neighbor function $k_{nn}(k)$ while simultaneously allowing to fix a priori an arbitrary degree distribution $P(k)$. Furthermore, an algorithm has been introduced generating arbitrary two-point correlated networks with an up to date unmatched efficiency and accuracy, which was previously unavailable. In collaboration with Andreas Pusch, the algorithm has been extended to incorporate the control over clustering. With the ability to control two-point correlations and clustering in networks, their impact on two dynamical processes has been analysed. The functional form of the average nearest neighbor function $k_{nn}(k)$ has been set to depend on one parameter, the correlation parameter α, which allows to tune two-point correlations from assortative over uncorrelated to disassortative two-point correlations. With the introduced metholodgy, virtually any dynamical process on a network can be systematically studied with respect to two-point correlations and clustering.

The first dynamical process considered belongs to the class of diffusion-annihilation dynamics, characterized by the stoichometric reaction equation $A + B \to \emptyset$. An analytical treatment in the case of uncorrelated networks has been performed. The analysis revealed an explicit dependence of the density decay on the network topology. In the long-time, low-density limit, the density decay in dependence of time becomes a power-law, such that $\rho^{-1} \propto t^f$. The value of f is equal to 1 for homogeneous networks with a finite second moment $\overline{k^2}$ of the degree distribution. In the case of scale-free networks with a scaling exponent γ in the range $(2,3]$, the second moment $\overline{k^2}$ diverges. This causes f to turn into an explicit function of the scaling exponent γ, which is $f = (\gamma - 2)^{-1}$, resulting in values of f greater than 1. Besides the density decay, the $A + B \to \emptyset$ reaction is characterized by pattern formation in the form of a segregation of the two components. On scale-free networks the segregation has been shown to be pronounced for disassortative networks in comparison to uncorrelated networks. Contrarily, these disassortative networks display a faster reaction speed than uncorrelated networks. Observing that the efficiency of the process is strongly increased for disassortative networks resolves this contradiction. Disassortative two-point correlated networks are capable to combine contradictory

5 Conclusion and Discussion

aims such as segregation and high reaction speed. The ability of disassortative networks to combine contradictory concerns appears to be a general feature of this topological property. For example, biological networks are subject to evolution under contrary concerns and are in most cases disassortative, i.e. protein interaction and gene regulation networks.

As a second dynamical process, the famous Prisoner's Dilemma game has been studied. The characteristics of the dynamics crucially depend on the implementation of the finite replicator dynamics analogue used. Accumulation of payoffs leads to an inertness of vertices with a high degree k which participate in many games. The inertness against strategy adoption ultimately supports the sustainment of cooperation and leads in the case of scale-free networks to a dominance of the cooperation strategy over the defect strategy. Exploiting the influence of two-point correlations in the accumulated payoff version shows that assortativity supports cooperation, especially in the domain of large values of the temptation to defect parameter b close to 2. In the case of networks with clustering, the enhancement of the cooperator density is even stronger than it is caused by assortative two-point correlations in the regime of the temptation to defect parameter b close to 2. This result is in accordance with the strong assortative two-point correlation patterns and strong clustering observed within social networks, suggesting the relevance of these topological properties with respect to the sustainment of cooperation for social networks.

An alternative version of the Prisoner's Dilemma has been considered as well. The implementation of the finite replicator dynamics analogue has been altered from utilizing accumulated payoffs to effective payoffs. The use of effective payoffs substantially changes the characteristics of the Prisoner's Dilemma dynamics. Scale-free networks exert an increased support of cooperation in comparison to Erdős-Rényi networks only in the regime of a highly challenging scenario, corresponding to a temptation to defect parameter b close to 2. Using effective payoffs almost removes the network topology from the dynamics. Every player i with a degree k_i in the network is put into the equivalent situation to participate in a Prisoner's Dilemma game carried out in a well-mixed population consisting out of k_i individuals. Exploiting the concept of finite evolutionary stable strategies allows to classify whether the degree k_i of a vertex i is accessible to the cooperation strategy or not. An impact of two-point correlations has been observable while further correlation patterns like clustering have been found to be not relevant. This highlights the relevance of two-point correlations in networks as it even influences the efficiency ruled Prisoner's Dilemma, a dynamical process which virtually removes the network topology by definition of its rules. The two-point correlations of a network ultimately controls the distribution of edges, giving two-point correlations their striking importance.

The network evolution recovered the outstanding role of high variability in the degree sequence of a network topology. High variability results in a strongly heterogeneous distribution of degrees and is realized by a scale-free network topology. A scale-free network with a power-law degree distribution has a second moment considerably larger than the mean degree. This combination ensures the overall connectedness of the network while providing a relatively low mean degree. A low mean degree ensures that dynamical systems are moved away from mean-field behavior as it was found for the Prisoner's Dilemma. On the other hand, the strong heterogeneity causes vertices of vastly different degrees to be connected. Thus, vertices of different scales become interwoven. For the example of the Prisoner's Dilemma, this ultimately amplifies the density of cooperation. The benefit for the reaction-diffusion system from the heterogeneity is the strong reduction of the average distance from every vertex to any other vertex. The degree heterogeneity is simultaneously of great importance for the topology and the dynamics of a network. However, for complex topologies to emerge, more than a bias towards degree heterogeneity is necessary, since the $A + B \rightarrow \emptyset$ process studied results in the trivial structure of a star which has a degree sequence variability scaling directly with the system size N.

In this Thesis the major results were drawn from a systematic study of two-point correlations and a network evolution. First, the evolution of networks driven by a selection method with respect to a dynamics requires a sufficiently complex dynamics and an adequate network mutation mechanism. Otherwise trivial networks will emerge or the dynamics is insensitive against mutations induced by the mutation mechanism. Second, while the degree distribution characterizes the vertices of a network, the two-point correlations of a network characterize the edges of a network and generally alter dynamical processes on networks.

A Appendix

A.1 Analytical Treatment of the Annihilation-Diffusion Process

We assume the complex network of N nodes to be fully defined by its $N \times N$ adjacency matrix a_{ij}. To discuss a physically meaningful complex network in the sense of diffusion, we take the network to be undirected and free of self- and multiple-connections. Therefore, a_{ij} is a traceless, symmetric binary matrix with the elements a_{ij} being 0 or 1, which symbols a (dis)connection between site i and j. The state of vertex i at time t is described by two dichotomous variables $n_i^{(a)}(t)$ and $n_i^{(b)}(t)$. Their values may be 1 or 0 only, indicating the presence or absence of a particle A ($n_i^{(a)}(t)$) and B ($n_i^{(b)}(t)$). The system state is thus defined by

$$\mathbf{n}(t) = \mathbf{n}^{(a)}(t) + \mathbf{n}^{(b)}(t)$$
$$\mathbf{n}^{(a)}(t) = \{n_1^{(a)}(t), n_2^{(a)}(t), ..., n_N^{(a)}(t)\} \quad (A.1)$$
$$\mathbf{n}^{(b)}(t) = \{n_1^{(b)}(t), n_2^{(b)}(t), ..., n_N^{(b)}(t)\}.$$

Note, that these variables have to fulfill the constraint $n_i^{(a)}(t)\, n_i^{(b)}(t) = 0$ at any time. In the course of the calculation, we will take the average over multiple realizations of the same system, turning the discrete $n_i^{(a)}(t)$ and $n_i^{(b)}(t)$ variables into densities $\rho_i^{(a)}(t)$ and $\rho_i^{(b)}(t)$. Furthermore, we will assume throughout the analysis the statistical equivalence of vertices of the same degree k. Therefore, denoting by $\mathcal{V}(k)$ the set of all vertices with the same degree k, we assume that

$$\rho_i^{(a)}(t) \equiv \rho_k^{(a)}(t) \quad \forall\, i \in \mathcal{V}(k)$$
$$\rho_i^{(b)}(t) \equiv \rho_k^{(b)}(t) \quad \forall\, i \in \mathcal{V}(k) \quad (A.2)$$

is valid. Following standard MF treatment, we hence neglect all fluctuations which might exist within a set of vertices $\mathcal{V}(k)$. The total density $\rho^{(a)}(t)$ ($\rho^{(b)}(t)$) is given by the set of partial particle densities $\{\rho_k^{(a)}(t)\}$ ($\{\rho_k^{(b)}(t)\}$) through the relation

$$\rho^{(a)}(t) = \sum_k \rho_k^{(a)}(t)\, P(k). \quad (A.3)$$

A Appendix

A dynamics starts by random assignment of maximal one particle per vertex. The particles diffuse by random jumps at a rate λ to adjacent neighbors through the network. If two different particles meet at a vertex, they instantly annihilate and the vertex becomes empty. Before we proceed to the time evolution of the system, we first derive an expression for the particle pair-correlations in dependence of the partial particle densities.

A.1.1 Particle pair-correlations

We quantify the particle pair-correlations for given partial particle densities by counting the number of contacts between particles on adjacent vertices. To count the AB contacts of a vertex i, we assume vertex i to carry an A particle and count the number of adjacent vertices which are occupied by a B particle. Setting this number in relation to all connections of the vertex i yields the pair-correlation coefficient

$$q_i^{(ab)}(t) = \frac{1}{k_i} n_i^{(a)}(t) \sum_j a_{ij} n_j^{(b)}(t). \qquad (A.4)$$

Averaging now over a whole ensemble of equal systems and making use of the usual MF assumption $\langle n_i^{(a)}(t) n_j^{(b)}(t) \rangle \approx \langle n_i^{(a)}(t) \rangle \cdot \langle n_j^{(b)}(t) \rangle$, we obtain

$$Q_i^{(ab)}(t) = \frac{1}{k_i} \rho_i^{(a)}(t) \sum_j a_{ij} \rho_j^{(b)}(t). \qquad (A.5)$$

By using the statistical equivalence of all N_k vertices i with the same degree k, we can sum over all these vertices such that

$$Q_k^{(ab)}(t) = \frac{1}{k} \rho_k^{(a)}(t) \sum_{k'} \rho_{k'}^{(b)}(t) \frac{1}{N_k} \sum_{i \in \mathcal{V}(k)} \sum_{j \in \mathcal{V}(k')} a_{ij}. \qquad (A.6)$$

In this step, we split the sum with index j into two sums over k' and one over $\mathcal{V}(k')$. The double sum over a_{ij} is related to the conditional probability $P(k'|k)$ that a vertex of given degree k has a neighbor which has degree k'. This equation has been derived previously [Boguñá et al., 2003] to be

$$\frac{1}{kN_k} \sum_{i \in \mathcal{V}(k)} \sum_{j \in \mathcal{V}(k')} a_{ij} = P(k'|k). \qquad (A.7)$$

Using this equation and assuming an uncorrelated network, which simplifies the conditional probability $P(k'|k)$ to $k' P(k')/\overline{k}$, we obtain the expression

$$Q_k^{(ab)}(t) = \rho_k^{(a)}(t) \langle \rho_k^{(b)}(t) \rangle. \qquad (A.8)$$

A.1 Analytical Treatment of the Annihilation-Diffusion Process

One should note that by introducing the mean $\overline{k}$, the values of the exponent γ are limited to $\gamma > 2$. Otherwise the mean $\overline{k}$ is not defined in the limit of infinite size networks ($N \to \infty$). The overall particle pair-correlation coefficient $Q_{AB}(t)$ can easily be computed by multiplying Eq. (A.8) with $P(k)$ and summing once more over all k,

$$Q_{AB}(t) = \rho^{(a)}(t) \langle \rho_k^{(b)}(t) \rangle. \quad (A.9)$$

Analogously, we have $Q^{(aa)}(t) = \rho^{(a)}(t) \langle \rho_k^{(a)}(t) \rangle$, $Q^{(bb)}(t) = \rho^{(b)}(t) \langle \rho_k^{(b)}(t) \rangle$, and $Q^{(ba)}(t) = \rho^{(b)}(t) \langle \rho_k^{(a)}(t) \rangle$.

A.1.2 Density decay

For further computations we will assume for simplicity that the initial densities of $\rho^{(a)}$ and $\rho^{(b)}$ are equal, so that there is a symmetry between A and B particles. We will calculate only an expression for $n^{(a)}(t)$, and one may obtain the corresponding $n^{(b)}(t)$ equations by interchanging indices A and B. Modeling the diffusion as a Poisson process [Kampen, 1992], the set of $\{n_i^{(a)}(t)\}$ changes within an infinitesimal time interval dt as

$$n_i^{(a)}(t + dt) = n_i^{(a)}(t)\, \eta_i^{(a)}(dt) + \left[1 - (n_i^{(a)}(t) + n_i^{(b)}(t))\right] \xi_i^{(a)}(dt). \quad (A.10)$$

Here $\eta_i^{(a)}$ and $\xi_i^{(a)}$ are dichotomous random variables, taking values of 0 or 1 with certain probabilities p and $1 - p$ respectively,

$$\eta_i^{(a)}(dt) = \begin{cases} 0 & p = \lambda\, dt \left[\sum_j \frac{a_{ij} n_j^{(b)}(t)}{k_j} + \left(1 - \frac{1}{k_i} \sum_j a_{ij} n_j^{(a)}(t)\right)\right] \\ 1 & 1 - p \end{cases} \quad (A.11)$$

$$\xi_i^{(a)}(dt) = \begin{cases} 1 & p = \lambda\, dt \sum_j \frac{a_{ij} n_j^{(a)}(t)}{k_j} \\ 0 & 1 - p \end{cases}. \quad (A.12)$$

The following two cases need to be distinguished: (i) If site i is occupied by an A particle at instant t, $\eta_i^{(a)}(dt)$ is responsible for the next time step: The site may become empty ($\eta_i^{(a)} = 0$) with a probability proportional to the product of the jumping rate λ and the time interval dt if a B particle in the neighborhood jumps onto site i or if the A particle at i jumps away to a neighborhood site where no A particle is already located. Otherwise no change happens. (ii) If the site i is empty at instant t, then $\xi_i^{(a)}(dt)$ will determine the time evolution: The vertex may become occupied by an A particle only if one in the neighborhood jumps onto vertex i. Note

77

A Appendix

that the two random variables $\eta_i^{(a)}$ and $\xi_i^{(a)}$ are hence not independent from each other, but we will treat them as independent (cf. [Catanzaro et al., 2005a]).

Equation (A.10) yields an average time evolution for $n_i^{(a)}(t)$

$$\langle n_i^{(a)}(t+\mathrm{d}t)\rangle = n_i^{(a)}(t) - \mathrm{d}t \left\{ n_i^{(a)}(t) + \sum_j \left[n_i^{(a)}(t) \frac{a_{ij} n_j^{(b)}(t)}{k_j} \right. \right.$$
$$- n_i^{(a)}(t) \frac{1}{k_i} a_{ij} n_j^{(a)}(t) \quad \text{(A.13)}$$
$$\left. \left. - \left(1 - [n_i^{(a)}(t) + n_i^{(b)}(t)]\right) \frac{a_{ij} n_j^{(a)}(t)}{k_j} \right] \right\},$$

where we have set without loss of generality the jumping rate $\lambda = 1$. Averaging over a whole set of equal initial configurations and applying once more Eq. (A.7) and the statistical equivalence of vertices with the same degree, Eq. (A.2), we obtain after some formal rearrangements

$$\frac{\mathrm{d}\rho_k^{(a)}}{\mathrm{d}t} = -\rho_k^{(a)} - \sum_{k'} \left\{ \frac{1}{k'} \left[\rho_k^{(a)} \rho_{k'}^{(b)} - k' \rho_k^{(a)} \frac{1}{k} \rho_{k'}^{(a)} \right. \right.$$
$$\left. \left. -\rho_{k'}^{(a)} + \rho_k^{(a)} \rho_{k'}^{(a)} + \rho_k^{(b)} \rho_{k'}^{(a)} \right] kP(k'|k) \right\}. \quad \text{(A.14)}$$

Here we have suppressed the explicit time dependence for the sake of simplicity. Assuming the network to be uncorrelated (i.e. that $P(k'|k) = k' P(k')/\overline{k}$) allows us to perform the sum over k', yielding finally the expression

$$\frac{\mathrm{d}\rho_k^{(a)}}{\mathrm{d}t} = -\rho_k^{(a)} - \frac{k}{\overline{k}} \left[\rho_k^{(a)} \rho^{(b)} - \rho^{(a)} + \rho_k^{(a)} \rho^{(a)} + \rho_k^{(b)} \rho^{(a)} \right] + \rho_k^{(a)} \langle \rho_k^{(a)} \rangle \quad \text{(A.15)}$$

for the partial particle densities. Multiplying Eq. (A.15) with $P(k)$ and summing over all k values results in the differential equation for the overall density,

$$\frac{\mathrm{d}\rho^{(a)}}{\mathrm{d}t} = -\rho^{(b)} \langle \rho_k^{(a)} \rangle - \rho^{(a)} \langle \rho_k^{(b)} \rangle$$
$$= -Q^{(ab)} - Q^{(ba)}. \quad \text{(A.16)}$$

From Eq. (A.16) it is apparent that the density decay is directly proportional to the pair-correlations among unlike particles. To proceed further, we need expressions for $\rho_k^{(a)}$ and $\rho_k^{(b)}$. Since the initial densities are equal, we have forcibly $Q^{(aa)} = Q^{(bb)}$ because of symmetry. This implies the equality $\rho_k^{(a)} = \rho_k^{(b)} \equiv \rho_k'$, allowing further

A.1 Analytical Treatment of the Annihilation-Diffusion Process

simplifications and transforming Eq. (A.15) into

$$\begin{aligned}\frac{d\rho'_k}{dt} &= -\rho'_k + \frac{k}{\overline{k}}[1-3\rho'_k]\rho' + \rho'_k\langle\rho'_k\rangle \\ &= -\rho'_k + \frac{k}{\overline{k}}[1-3\rho'_k]\rho' + Q''_k.\end{aligned} \quad (A.17)$$

The further derivation of the partial particle densities is discussed in Sec. 3.1.1, enlightening the impact of 'jamming'.

A.1.3 Validation of the approximations

To validate the analytical calculations developed, we have to verify the two central approximations made which are based on the assumption of a small particle density on the network. Furthermore, it is crucial to get an estimate which densities can be considered small enough for the validity of the approximations. Our first approximation was to neglect in Eq. (A.15) the 'jamming' term Q''_k in comparison to the other term quadratic in the density $3k\rho'_k\rho'/\overline{k}$. We have shown the validity of this approximation analytically for vertices with a degree $k \gg k_c$ and $k \ll k_c$ (the latter for low densities). To check the intermediate range $k \approx k_c$, we perform numerical simulations. If we set the ratio in Eq. (3.7) equal to 1, we obtain a critical degree $\tilde{k}_c$,

$$\tilde{k}_c = \frac{\langle\rho'_k\rangle}{3\rho'/\overline{k}}, \quad (A.18)$$

which separates vertices whose 'jamming' term is less important than the other quadratic density term in Eq. (A.17) from those vertices for which the 'jamming' term is at least of equal importance. The time-evolution of the particle density on vertices with a degree $k \gg \tilde{k}_c$ is not affected by 'jamming', whereas vertices with a degree of the order of $\tilde{k}_c$ or lower are affected. On the other hand vertices with a small degree do not contribute to the overall particle density at later times, since the hubs dynamically attract the particles and carry the highest density $\rho'_c = 1/3$. Considering only vertices as hubs which have a degree $k > k_c = \overline{k}/3\rho'$, we have as a condition for 'jamming' not being relevant

$$\tilde{k}_c \ll k_c. \quad (A.19)$$

If condition (A.19) is fulfilled, there are no vertices left in the network which do carry a sufficiently high density and whose 'jamming' term is important for the time-evolution of their $\rho_k(t)$. In Fig. A.1 we exemplified this condition for an exponent $\gamma = 2.75$ and an initial particle density $\rho_0 = 0.95$. Note that the curves are only drawn until k_c reaches the value of the maximum degree $k_{\max}$ present in the

A Appendix

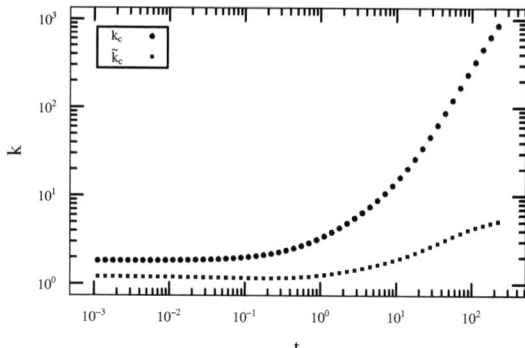

Figure A.1: Plot of k_c and $\tilde{k}_c$ of the numerically simulated $A + B \to \emptyset$ process for an exponent $\gamma = 2.75$ and an initial density $\rho_0 = 0.95$. Since k_c is increasing much faster than $\tilde{k}_c$, 'jamming' becomes quickly irrelevant.

network. Once the value of k_c is much greater than $\tilde{k}_c$ the 'jamming' effect is of no more relevance for the time evolution of the process for all vertices in the network, including those with $k \approx k_c$. It is crucial to note that k_c grows much faster than $\tilde{k}_c$ in the course of the process. Therefore, the 'jamming' is continuously diminishing during the dynamics and only important for low degree vertices carrying a high density in the beginning of the process. An equivalent criterion to test whether 'jamming' is not relevant is to check if the ratio of $\tilde{k}_c/k_c$ is substantially smaller than 1. In Fig. A.2(a) we illustrate this for an initial density $\rho_0 = 0.95$. Again, the individual curves are only drawn until k_c reaches $k_{\max}$. They start with a maximum value of almost 1, indicating the presence of 'jamming' and drop quite quickly well below 1. In Fig. A.2(b) we show the same simulations but with a much smaller initial density of $\rho_0 = 0.1$. Most importantly, these curves already begin at values well below 1 and therefore there is never 'jamming' present in the dynamics. The interesting intermediate increase of $\tilde{k}_c/k_c$ for the initial density $\rho_0 = 0.1$ (Fig. A.2(b)) comes from the fact the dynamical hubs start with a density $\rho'_0 = 0.05$ which is smaller than their long-time density $\rho'_c = 1/3$. Therefore, all vertices with $\rho'_k < 1/3$ and a degree $k > k_c$ will have increasing particle densities ρ'_k which enter $\langle \rho'_k \rangle$ in Eq. (A.18). Once the dynamics has reached its long-time behavior, there are no more ρ'_k-terms in $\langle \rho'_k \rangle$ which increase in magnitude, since the dynamical hubs carry the highest density in the network.

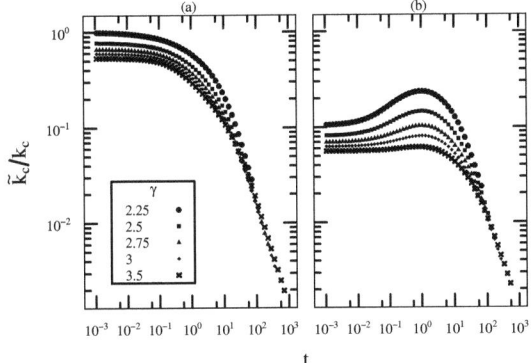

Figure A.2: Ratio of $\tilde{k}_c$ and k_c of the numerically simulated $A + B \to \emptyset$ process on networks of different exponents γ as indicated, with an initial particle density (a) $\rho_0 = 0.95$ and (b) $\rho_0 = 0.1$.

The second approximation made to obtain an expression for ρ'_k, the quasi-static assumption $d\rho_k^{(a)}/dt \approx 0$, yielded Eq. (3.11). Rearranging Eq. (3.11) into

$$k \left(\frac{1}{\rho'_k} - 3 \right) = \frac{\overline{k}}{\rho'} \tag{A.20}$$

leads to an expression where the right hand side (and consequently the left hand side as well) is independent of k if the approximation is indeed valid. Plotting the left hand side of Eq. (A.20) for a couple different degrees k should yield a data-collapse onto a single curve. Fig. A.3 on the following page illustrates this in the case of an exponent $\gamma = 2.5$. The curves join quite nicely at roughly $t \approx 50$. Similar time points are obtained for other exponents γ. We can therefore expect that the quasi-static approximation holds after this time.

A.2 Numerical Methods

A.2.1 Generation of Two-Point Correlated Networks

The overall scheme of the algorithm to construct a network with N vertices and a given joint degree distribution $P(j, k)$ is the following:

A Appendix

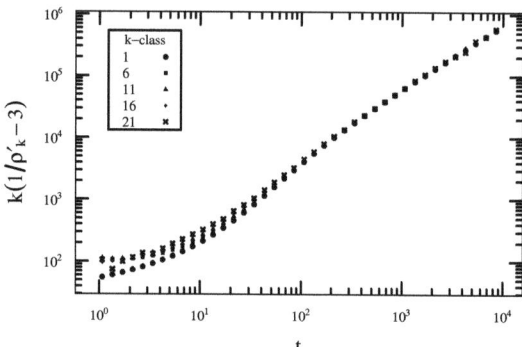

Figure A.3: Numerical validation of the quasi-static approximation according to Eq. (A.20) for the $A + B \to \emptyset$ process, exemplified by an exponent $\gamma = 2.5$ and an initial density $\rho_0 = 0.1$. The k-classes are logarithmically joined, where class 1 corresponds to vertices of degree $k = 2$, class 6 to $8 \leq k \leq 10$, class 11 to $33 \leq k \leq 42$, class 16 to $134 \leq k \leq 178$, and class 21 to $563 \leq k \leq 750$. A data-collapse is observed for $t \gtrsim 50$.

1. As in the CM algorithm, one first has to draw a degree sequence by calculating the theoretical (continuous) edge end distribution $P_e(k)$ from the joint degree distribution $P(j,k)$ and transform that into a degree distribution $P(k)$. From this distribution, a degree sequence of length N is drawn.

2. Each element of the degree sequence represents a vertex. All vertices with the same degree k are then sorted into degree classes, each containing only vertices of the same degree k.

3. To compensate for discretization effects caused by the finiteness of the sampled network, one has to calculate the discrete edge end distribution $P_e^{(d)}(k)$ from the generated degree sequence. To do so, one acquires, by estimating the size of each degree class, the discrete degree distribution $P^{(d)}(k)$, which corresponds to a discrete edge end distribution by $P_e^{(d)}(k) = k\, P^{(d)}(k)/\bar{k}$.

4. Next, the discrete conditional probability $P^{(d)}(j|k)$ is setup. To obtain a matrix which accommodates the discretization effects, one replaces the continuous edge end distributions $P_e(k)$ in the definition of the conditional probability distribution of Eq. (2.5) by the discrete edge end distributions $P_e^{(d)}(k)$ and obtains

therefore
$$\begin{aligned}P(j|k) = \frac{P(j,k)}{P_e(k)} &= P_e(j)\,f(j,k) \\ &\approx P_e^{(d)}(j)\,f(j,k) = P_e^{(d)}(j)\,\frac{P(j,k)}{P_e(j)\,P_e(k)}.\end{aligned} \qquad (A.21)$$

Since the discrete edge end distribution $P_e^{(d)}(j)$ and the continous correlation function $f(j,k)$ is mixed, the resulting conditional degree distribution $P^{(d)}(j|k)$ is only approximately normalized for a given degree class k. To obtain a conditional probability distribution suitable for sampling degree classes, one normalizes each degree class separately, leading to the final form

$$P^{(d)}(j|k) = \frac{P_e^{(d)}(j)}{P_e(j)}\,P(j,k)\left(\sum_j \frac{P_e^{(d)}(j)}{P_e(j)}\,P(j,k)\right)^{-1}. \qquad (A.22)$$

This definition is consistent with the limes $N \to \infty$, as the discrete edge end distribution $P_e^{(d)}(j)$ becomes equal in this limit to the continous edge end distribution $P_e(j)$ and the ratios $P_e^{(d)}(j)/P_e(j)$ become exactly 1, respectively.

5. After all base data structures have been initialized, the algorithm starts to draw edges by drawing edge ends. The first edge end is selected by first drawing a degree class k from the edge end distribution $P_e^{(d)}(k)$ and then randomly choose a vertex from that degree class.

6. The second end of the edge is chosen in the same two step manner. However, the second draw of a degree class j is done with the appropriate conditional probability distribution $P^{(d)}(j|k)$ instead of the edge end distribution $P_e^{(d)}(k)$. This construction scheme yields correctly correlated graphs, since it is

$$\underbrace{P_e(k)}_{\text{1. draw}}\underbrace{P(j|k)}_{\text{2. draw}} = P(j,k). \qquad (A.23)$$

An edge is created whenever the constraints of neither self- nor multiple-edges is met. Otherwise the drawn edge is rejected and the algorithm continues with step five.

7. If the edge is created, the probability weights of the two edge ends are removed from the corresponding degree classes in the edge end distribution $P_e^{(d)}(k)$ and the conditional probability distribution matrix $P^{(d)}(j|k)$. The removal of the probability weight is equivalent to the removal of the two half-edges from the list of eligible half-edges in the CM algorithm.

8. The steps five to seven are repeated until no edge ends are left and all edges are formed.

A Appendix

The principal numerical costs of the algorithm arises from the continuous sampling of degree classes in the steps five and six above. Since the algorithm has to sample only the degree classes actually realized, which is a significant lower number than the system size N, the numerical costs are of the order $\mathcal{O}(N^\alpha)$ with $\alpha < 1$. Furthermore, due to the removal of probability weight of used half-edges throughout the construction procedure, the algorithm samples only the possible configuration space which remains valid in each iteration step just as in the CM algorithm. The memory usage of the algorithm scales with the square of the number of realized degree classes. This can become a significant advantage over the CM procedure as described above, since the memory usage of the CM procedure scales with the number of half-edges needed to construct the network.

A.2.2 Generation of Two-Point Correlated Networks with Clustering

The scheme of the algorithm to construct a network with N vertices and given discrete versions of corresponding distributions, $P_d(j,k)$ and $c_d(k)$, $P_d(j,k)$ being the number of connections between vertices with degrees k and j (double that number if $k = j$), and $c_d(k)$ being the number of triangle edges constituted by vertices with degree k, is the following:

1. One begins by assigning a number of stubs (the target degree) to every vertex according to the degree distribution $P_d(k)$, which is calculated from $P_d(j,k)$ as $P_d(k) = \sum_j P_d(j,k)/k$.

2. The next step is to get a list of degrees of triangle-corners, which shall contain $c_d(k)$ entries with value k. For every connection built the appropriate entry in the $P_d(j,k)$ matrix is decreased by 1 and for every triangle built (for every connection placed, a check is performed for simultaneous neighbors of the involved vertices as any shared neighbor accounts for a new triangle built) to delete one entry from the triangle list and to decrease $c_d(k)$ by 1 for every degree involved.

3. Then one starts to build all triangles in the triangle list one by one. Let v_i be the vertices involved and k_i their target degree.

4. Draw a random entry k_1 from the triangle list and draw a corresponding vertex v_1 with at least one free stub. If no such vertex is available, all entries with value k_1 are deleted from the triangle list and one starts again with this step.

5. Now, one chooses with uniform probability either (a) an edge or (b) a stub of vertex v_1 out of a list created by omitting all edges for whose end vertex no

A.2 Numerical Methods

more triangles can be build (i.e. $c_d(k) = 0$). In case of (a), one has chosen an edge and the end vertex is v_2. If a stub has been drawn (b), a vertex v_2 in the same manner is obtained as the vertex v_1 has been sampled with the further condition $P_d(k_1, k_2) > 0$. If it is not possible to find a k_2 fulfilling this condition, all entries with value k_1 are deleted from the triangle list and the algorithm starts again at step 4.

6. Next, one draws (a) an edge or (b) a stub of vertex v_2 from a list like one did in the preceding step for vertex v_1, but with edges inserted into the list only if they are fulfilling the supplementary condition of $P_d(k_1, k_3) > 0$ or vertex v_3 being connected to vertex v_1 and vertices v_1, v_2, and v_3 not already constituting a triangle. Having drawn an edge (a), the triangle is closed by adding the missing edges and updating all dynamic quantities. Having drawn a stub (b), a k_3 is choosen from the triangle list consistent with k_1 and k_2. It might happen that this is not possible and one starts again with step 4. When a k_3 is obtained, one draws a vertex v_3 which either has enough free stubs or is already connected to vertex v_1 or v_2, add the missing edges, and update all dynamic quantities.

Note that in steps 5 and 6 the case of two or three degrees being the same has to be properly taken into account in order not to build too much triangles or connections, and that self-connections are forbidden.

Those steps are repeated until no more triangles can be build anymore. This point may be defined by a maximum number of successive tries that did not result in a triangle being built or until the triangle list is empty.

Afterwards the rest of the graph is built by randomly choosing edges out of the remaining edge list, which contains $P_d(k_1, k_2)$ entries (k_1, k_2) for all degrees k_1, k_2. Two non-identical vertices are randomly choosen with stubs left and the edges (if the vertices are not already connected) are build which become deleted from the edge list. We repeat this until the edge list is empty or no more vertices are available which still lack connections and are not already connected to each other. If there are edges left over (typically there is no edge left, and very seldomly there are more than one or two edges left), these are substituted by randomly connecting vertices.

A.2.3 Annihilation-Diffusion Dynamics

The $A + B \to \emptyset$ dynamics is simulated in the following way: Initially a fraction $\rho = 2\rho^{(a)} = 2\rho^{(b)}$ of randomly chosen vertices is selected. Then, the algorithm assigns randomly an equal amount of A and B particles to the set of chosen vertices.

A Appendix

Each vertex is assigned at most one particle. After this initial setup, the diffusion-annihilation dynamics starts. First, a vertex which carries a particle and a random adjacent neighbor of this vertex are randomly selected. Three cases need to be distinguished: (i) If the neighbor vertex is empty, the particle moves to the new vertex, leaving the initial vertex empty. (ii) If the neighbor vertex is occupied by a particle of the other type, an annihilation reaction occurs and both vertices become empty. Accordingly, the number of particles is decreased for each particle type by one, $n^{(a)} \to n^{(a)} - 1$, and $n^{(b)} \to n^{(b)} - 1$. (iii) If the neighbor vertex is occupied by a particle of the same type, then no jump occurs. In any case, the time is updated by $t \to t + 1/(n^{(a)} + n^{(b)})$, where $n^{(a)}$ and $n^{(b)}$ correspond to the values before the diffusion step, and one continues by selecting randomly another vertex carrying a particle, and so forth.

In order to obtain the system's typical behavior, in this Thesis averages of 50 independent dynamics on each graph and over 100 independent graphs are taken, making up a total of 5000 dynamics per data-point.

A.2.4 Prisoner's Dilemma Dynamics

The prisoner's dilemma dynamics is implemented similarly as by Gomez-Gardenes et al. [2007a]: (i) At the beginning, each individual i of the population (i.e., each node i) has the same probability of choosing cooperation or defection as initial strategy. (ii) Following Nowak et al. [2004], Santos & Pacheco [2005], the prisoner's dilemma payoffs are set as $R = 1$, $P = S = 0$, and $T \equiv b > 1$, so that the benefit b is the only parameter, and implement a finite population analogue of the replicator dynamics: At each time step t, which represents one generation of the discrete evolutionary time, each node i in the network plays with all its k_i neighbors and accumulates its obtained payoff π_i. Then, all individuals i update synchronously their strategies s_i by each one choosing one of its neighbors at random, say j, and comparing their respective payoffs π_i and π_j (π_i/k_i and π_j/k_j for the effective payoff dynamics). If the neighbor's payoff is lower or equal, then the individual i keeps its strategy s_i for the next time step. On the contrary, if the neighbor's payoff is higher, $\pi_j > \pi_i$, i adopts the strategy s_j of j for the next time step with probability $P(s_i \to s_j) = (\pi_j - \pi_i)/(b\max\{k_i, k_j\})$ for the cummulative and $P(s_i \to s_j) = (\pi_j/k_j - \pi_i/k_i)/b$ for the effective payoff version. In this Thesis, the dynamics is run for a transient time of 5000 generations. Then, the cooperator density is measured, the dynamics is evolved for another 1000 time steps, and the cooperator density is measured again. If both densities, each averaged over 10 time steps and separated by 1000 generations, deviate by more than 0.01, the procedure is repeated another 1000 generations later. Otherwise, the actual measurement is started over the next

10^4 time steps. All data presented in this Thesis is averaged over 100 network realizations with 50 independent dynamics with different initial conditions on each network realization, resulting in 5000 dynamics per data-point.

Bibliography

Ahn, Y.-Y., Jeong, H., Masuda, N., & Noh, J. D. (2006). Epidemic dynamics of two species of interacting particles on scale-free networks. *Phys. Rev. E*, *74*, 066113.

Albert, R., & Barabási, A.-L. (2002). Statistical mechanics of complex networks. *Rev. Mod. Phys.*, *74*, 47.

Albert, R., Jeong, H., & Barabási, A.-L. (1999). Internet: Diameter of the world-wide web. *Nature*, *401*, 130.

Barabási, A.-L., & Albert, R. (1999). Emergence of scaling in random networks. *Science*, *286*(5439), 509.

Binder, K., & Heermann, D. (1997). *Monte Carlo simulation in statistical physics*. Springer.

Boguñá, M., Pastor-Satorras, R., & Vespignani, A. (2003). Absence of epidemic threshold in scale-free networks with degree correlations. *Phys. Rev. Lett.*, *90*, 028701.

Boguñá, M., Pastor-Satorras, R., & Vespignani, A. (2003). Epidemic spreading in complex networks with degree correlations. In R. Pastor-Satorras, M. Rubi, & A. Diaz-Guilera (Eds.) *Statistical Mechanics of Complex Networks*, vol. 625 of *Lecture Notes in Physics*. Springer Verlag, Berlin.

Boguñá, M., Pastor-Satorras, R., & Vespignani, A. (2004). Cut-offs and finite size effects in scale-free networks. *Eur. Phys. J. B*, *38*, 205–209.

Bollobas, B. (1980). *Eur. J. Comb.*, *1*, 311.

Catanzaro, M., Boguna, M., & Pastor-Satorras, R. (2005a). Diffusion-annihilation processes in complex networks. *Phys. Rev. E*, *71*, 056104.

Catanzaro, M., Boguñá, M., & Pastor-Satorras, R. (2005b). Generation of uncorrelated random scale-free networks. *Phys. Rev. E*, *71*(2), 027103.

Bibliography

Cohen, R., Erez, K., ben Avraham, D., & Havlin, S. (2000). Resilience of the internet to random breakdowns. *Phys. Rev. Lett.*, *85*, 4626–4628.

Cohen, R., & Havlin, S. (2003). Scale-free networks are ultrasmall. *Phys. Rev. Lett.*, *90*, 058701.

Dorogovtsev, S., Mendes, J., Povolotsky, A., & Samukhin, A. (2005a). Organization of complex networks without multiple connections. *Phys. Rev. Lett.*, *95*, 195701.

Dorogovtsev, S., & Mendes, J. F. F. (2002). Evolution of networks. *Adv. Phys.*, *51*, 1079.

Dorogovtsev, S. N. (2004). Clustering of correlated networks. *Phys. Rev. E*, *69*, 027104.

Dorogovtsev, S. N., Goltsev, A. V., & Mendes, J. F. F. (2002). Ising model on networks with an arbitrary distribution of connections. *Phys. Rev. E*, *66*, 016104.

Dorogovtsev, S. N., Goltsev, A. V., & Mendes, J. F. F. (2005b). Correlations in interacting systems with a network topology. *Phys. Rev. E*, *72*, 066130.

Dorogovtsev, S. N., Mendes, J. F. F., & Samukhin, A. N. (2001). Size-dependent degree distribution of a scale-free growing network. *Phys. Rev. E*, *63*, 062101.

Erdős, P., & Rényi, A. (1959). On random graphs. *Publ. Math.*, *6*, 290–297.

Erdős, P., & Rényi, A. (1960). On the evolution of random graphs. *Publ. Inst. Hung. Acad. Sci.*, *5*, 17–61.

Erdős, P., & Rényi, A. (1961). On the strength of connectedness of a random graph. *A. Math. Sci. Hungary*, *12*, 261–267.

Evlampiev, K., & Isambert, H. (2008). Conservation and topology of protein interaction networks under duplication-divergence evolution. *Proc. Nat. Acad. Sci.*, *105*, 9863–9868.

Gallos, L., & Argyrakis, P. (2004). Absence of kinetic effects in reaction-diffusion processes in scale-free network. *Phys. Rev. Lett.*, *92*, 138301.

Gallos, L., & Argyrakis, P. (2005). Reaction-diffusion processes on correlated and uncorrelated scale-free networks. *Phys. Rev. E*, *72*.

Gomez-Gardenes, J., Campillo, M., Floria, L. M., & Moreno, Y. (2007a). Dynamical organization of cooperation in complex topologies. *Phys. Rev. Lett.*, *98*, 108103.

Gomez-Gardenes, J., Moreno, Y., & Arenas, A. (2007b). Paths to synchronization on complex networks. *Phys. Rev. Lett.*, *98*, 034101.

Gross, T., D'Lima, C. J. D., & Blasius, B. (2006). Epidemic dynamics on an adaptive network. *Phys. Rev. Lett.*, *96*, 208701.

Kampen, N. V. (1992). *Stochastic Processes in Physics and Chemistry*. Elsevier.

Lee, J.-S., Goh, K.-I., Kahng, B., & Kim, D. (2006). Intrinsic degree-correlations in the static model of scale-free networks. *Eur. Phys. J. B*, *49*, 231–238.

Li, L., Alderson, D., Doyle, J., & Willinger, W. (2006). Towards a theory of scale-free graphs: Definition, properties, and implications. *Intern. Math.*, *2*, 431–523.

Maynard Smith, J. (1974). Theory of games and the evolution of animal contests. *J. Theor. Biol.*, *47*, 209–221.

Maynard Smith, J. (1982). *Evolution and the theory of games*. Cambridge University Press.

Maynard Smith, J., & Price, G. (1973). The logic of animal conflict. *Nature*, *246*(5427), 15–18.

Molloy, M., & Reed, B. (1995). A critical point for random graphs with a given degree sequence. *Rand. Struct. Alg.*, *6*, 161–179.

Molloy, M., & Reed, B. (1998). The size of the largest component of a random graph on a fixed degree sequence. *Comb., Prob. and Comp.*, *7*, 295–306.

Nash, J. (1950a). Equilibrium points in n-person games. *Proc. Natl. Acad. Sci. USA*, *36*, 48–49.

Nash, J. (1950b). *Non cooperative games*. Ph.D. thesis, Princeton University.

Nash, J. (1951). Non-cooperative games. *Ann. Math.*, *54*(2), 286–295.

Newman, M. E. J. (2002). Assortative mixing in networks. *Phys. Rev. Lett.*, *89*, 208701.

Newman, M. E. J. (2003a). Properties of highly clustered networks. *Phys. Rev. E*, *68*, 026121.

Newman, M. E. J. (2003b). The structure and function of complex networks. *SIAM Rev.*, *45*, 167.

Nowak, M. (2006). *Evolutionary Dynamics*. Harvard University Press.

Bibliography

Nowak, M. A., Sasaki, A., Taylor, C., & Fudenberg, D. (2004). Emergence of cooperation and evolutionary stability in finite populations. *Nature*, *428*(6983), 646–650.

Pastor-Satorras, R., & Vespignani, A. (2004). *Evolution and Structure of the Internet: A Statistical Physics Approach*. Cambridge University Press.

Pusch, A., Weber, S., & Porto, M. (2008a). Generating random networks with given degree-degree correlations and degree-dependent clustering. *Phys. Rev. E*, *77*, 017101.

Pusch, A., Weber, S., & Porto, M. (2008b). Impact of topology on the dynamical organization of cooperation in the prisoner's dilemma game. *Phys. Rev. E*, *77*, 036120.

Santos, F. C., & Pacheco, J. M. (2005). Scale-free networks provide a unifying framework for the emergence of cooperation. *Phys. Rev. Lett.*, *95*, 098104.

Sella, G., & Hirsh, A. (2005). The application of statistical physics to evolutionary biology. *Proc. Natl. Acad. Sci. USA*, *102*, 9541–9546.

Serrano, M. A., & Boguñá, M. (2005). Tuning clustering in random networks with arbitrary degree distributions. *Phys. Rev. E*, *72*, 036133.

Song, C., Havlin, S., & Makse, H. A. (2005). Self-similarity of complex networks. *Nature*, *433*, 392–395.

Song, C., Havlin, S., & Makse, H. A. (2006). Origins of fractality in the growth of complex networks. *Nature Phys.*, *2*, 275–281.

Szolnoki, A., Perc, M., & Danku, Z. (2008). Towards effective payoffs in the prisoner's dilemma game on scale-free networks. *Physica A*, *387*, 2075–2082.

Taylor, P. (1979). Evolutionarily stable strategies with two types of player. *J. App. Prob.*, *16*(1), 76–83.

Tomassini, M., Luthi, L., & Pestelacci, E. (2007). Social dilemmas and cooperation in complex networks. *Int. J. Mod. Phys. C*, *17*, 1173–1185.

Torney, D., & McConnell, H. (1983). Diffusion-limited reaction rate theory for two-dimensional systems. *Proc. R. Soc. Lond. A*, *387*, 147–170.

Toussaint, D., & Wilczek, F. (1983). Particle-antiparticle annihilation in diffusive motion. *J. Chem. Phys.*, *78*, 2642–2647.

Watts, D. J., & Strogatz, S. H. (1998). Collective dynamics of 'small-world' networks. *Nature*, *393*, 440.

Weber, S., Hütt, M.-T., & Porto, M. (2008). Pattern formation and efficiency of reaction-diffusion processes on complex networks. *Europhys. Lett.*, *82*(2), 28003.

Weber, S., & Porto, M. (2006). Multicomponent reaction-diffusion processes on complex networks. *Phys. Rev. E*, *74*, 046108.

Weber, S., & Porto, M. (2007). Generation of arbitrarily two-point-correlated random networks. *Phys. Rev. E*, *76*, 046111.

Weber, S., & Porto, M. (2009a). Efficiency based strategy spreading in the prisoner's dilemma game. *Eur. Phys. J. B*.

Weber, S., & Porto, M. (2009b). Modifying complex networks: Ergodic diffusion in network space. *in preparation*.

Weibull, J. W. (1995). *Evolutionary Game Theory*. MIT Press.

Xulvi-Brunet, R., & Sokolov, I. M. (2004). Reshuffling scale-free networks: From random to assortative. *Phys. Rev. E*, *70*, 066102.

Yule, G. U. (1925). A mathematical theory of evolution, based on the conclusions of Dr. JC Willis, frs. *Phil. Trans. R. Soc. of Lond. B*, *213*, 21–87.

List of Publications

Weber, S. and Porto, M. Multicomponent reaction-diffusion processes on complex networks. *Phys. Rev. E*, 74:046108, 2006.

Weber, S. and Porto, M. Generation of arbitrarily two-point-correlated random networks. *Phys. Rev. E*, 76:046111, 2007.

Pusch, A., Weber, S., and Porto, M. Generating random networks with given degree-degree correlations and degree-dependent clustering. *Phys. Rev. E*, 77:017101, 2008a.

Pusch, A., Weber, S., and Porto, M. Impact of topology on the dynamical organization of cooperation in the prisoner's dilemma game. *Phys. Rev. E*, 77:036120, 2008b.

Weber, S., Hütt, M.-T., and Porto, M. Pattern formation and efficiency of reaction-diffusion processes on complex networks. *Europhys. Lett.*, 82(2):28003, 2008.

Weber, S. and Porto, M. Efficiency based strategy spreading in the prisoner's dilemma game. *Eur. Phys. J. B*, 2009a. doi: 10.1140/epjb/e2009-00177-4.

Weber, S. and Porto, M. Modifying complex networks: Ergodic diffusion in network space. *in preparation*, 2009b.

Acknowledgements

I wish to express my thanks to numerous people who have provided me with support along the path leading this Thesis. Of value I can merely express has been the help of Prof. Dr. Markus Porto to me. He gave me the opportunity to realize this Thesis and it has always been a pleasure to work with him. From his guidance I have benefited professionally and personally in the course of this Thesis. Very much I appreciate the outstanding willingness to contribute at any time, his office door has always been open to me.

My special thanks go to Prof. Dr. Marc-Thorsten Hütt. From the collaboration with him I gained many helpful discussions and valuable comments. I would also like to thank Andreas Pusch who worked with me during his diploma thesis and has been of great value to the projects we shared.

For the many concerns one comes about in the course of a Thesis, I shared many helpful discussions with my colleagues Torben Jabben and Sebastian Schmitt. Especially I want to mention Florian Teichert and Katrin Wolff, both actively participated in creating this document by valuable proof reading.

Throughout my life my loving family, Ioana Popp-Weber, Willi Weber, and Franziska Weber, has always been there for me in any situation. I gratefully thank for the support and love I receive.

It is beyond words to thank my partner Nada Sissouno. Writing this Thesis surely required a great amount of understanding and I very much appreciate her caring and support.

Die VDM Verlagsservicegesellschaft sucht für wissenschaftliche Verlage abgeschlossene und herausragende

Dissertationen, Habilitationen, Diplomarbeiten, Master Theses, Magisterarbeiten usw.

für die kostenlose Publikation als Fachbuch.

Sie verfügen über eine Arbeit, die hohen inhaltlichen und formalen Ansprüchen genügt, und haben Interesse an einer honorarvergüteten Publikation?

Dann senden Sie bitte erste Informationen über sich und Ihre Arbeit per Email an *info@vdm-vsg.de*.

Sie erhalten kurzfristig unser Feedback!

VDM Verlagsservicegesellschaft mbH
Dudweiler Landstr. 99
D - 66123 Saarbrücken
www.vdm-vsg.de

Telefon +49 681 3720 174
Fax +49 681 3720 1749

Die VDM Verlagsservicegesellschaft mbH vertritt

Printed by Books on Demand GmbH, Norderstedt / Germany